MW00397809

THE CONVERSATION CONTINUES

by G. Walter Bush

Text copyright © 2015 G. Walter Bush

All Rights Reserved

For all those who purchased, shared, reviewed,
or promoted the first book.
Without you, there wouldn't have been a second.

TABLE OF CONTENTS

PREFACE

Welcome back to the conversation. That's what this is…my contribution to the ongoing discussion brewing all over the Internet, and therefore all over the globe. At this writing, citizens from no fewer than 21 countries have read *Unpacking "Chuck"*, and many more nations are represented on the "Chuck"-related sites and message boards spread across cyberspace. For reasons I can't quite fathom given the enduring popularity of the show, there are still no other books to consult: these two volumes remain the only ones written on the series. Whether you find yourself agreeing or disagreeing with what I observe in the text, my hope is that reading both *Unpacking "Chuck"* and *Unpacking "Chuck" 2.0* will at least spur your thinking and leave you pondering the series in ways that you didn't before. Indeed, the most important aspect is that the conversation is continuing about a series that remains worth talking about more than three years after the end of the initial broadcast.

So what exactly is *Unpacking "Chuck" 2.0*? In many ways, it is similar to the 1.0. This is a literary analysis of the dramatic elements of the audio-visual text, not the actors, the acting (unless it affects meaning) or solely comic elements of the show. Moreover, the purpose of this analysis is limited to interpreting the text, not to criticize or praise it (with only occasional exceptions, including the last chapter). Therefore, unlike a blog, the tone will remain predominately objective, though I hope you still sense the passion. These readings will again show some variety in focus, too: half consist of character analyses, while the other half covers episode, arc, theme, and technical discussions. The philosophical approach will continue to emphasize form and structure as well, treating the text primarily as an independent object that evidences internal harmony. Whenever possible, I allow the text to interpret itself. If you're only seeking connections to elements outside the text, particularly implied pop culture links, this book won't be your cup of tea.

But there are significant differences, too. The material in this sequel is new; references to ideas in the first book are almost always either reframed or provided as context to inform the fresh point at hand. Additionally, while the original volume dealt mainly with Team Bartowski, this companion expands the analytic scope to include all major auxiliary characters and the series' two most prominent villains while also addressing some key elements pertaining to Chuck and Sarah not addressed in 1.0. To be honest, I found myself surprised by the depth of development evident in the portrayal of the auxiliary characters, much of which I had not detected before (I confess I wasn't really looking closely the first time). The same texturing applied to central characters extends to the supporting cast.

I'd like to thank those partly responsible for the writing of this book. There would have been nothing to write about were it not for the collective efforts of many in constructing an impressively textured and largely coherent audio-visual text over the course of five seasons despite facing many variables. From co-creators Josh Schwartz and Chris Fedak to the stable of talented writers, directors, and actors they corralled, and even the camera and lighting technicians: each played roles in the formation of the final product down to the fine and often important details. They succeeded in creating a show demonstrating profound range and depth that can be enjoyed as much for pure entertainment as its subtle sophistication. I would also be remiss if I didn't mention my gratitude for the many hours put in by "Beebs", my proof editor, and the creative talent at KB Design for the cover design and lay-out of the book.

If you feel that *Unpacking "Chuck" 2.0* merits a good review on Amazon, I'd appreciate it if you left one. The number of reviews posted the first go-round was a very small fraction of the number purchased. Please also consider liking the *Unpacking "Chuck"* page on Facebook and following me on Twitter @G_Walterbush for future appearances and projects.

- G.Walter Bush
  May 2015

Chapter 1: The Intersect: Part I

The Configuration of Mr. Roboto

Nine. No fewer than nine different characters download a version of the Intersect in five seasons of "Chuck" and survive sane enough to tell of it. Two more die on the verge of obtaining it. Some download relatively primitive prototypes of the secret government program; others download increasingly advanced versions. Some seek it for righteous purposes; some for ill. Some access it unwittingly; others intentionally. One even does both. The long and varied history of the Intersect makes for compelling and metaphor-filled theater, a pageant in which Chuck eventually takes—and remains—center stage.

The details surrounding the origins of the Intersect remain a tad hazy even after sifting through a series' worth of evidence. One point, however, clearly emerges: Chuck's father was the primary force in a collective effort to develop the Intersect's early versions. Ironically, Orion's own testimony on the matter leaves a bit of ambiguity. On one hand, when Chuck marvels, "I can't believe this. My father invented the Intersect," his dad doesn't accept all the recognition, replying, "Well, that's not true. I didn't invent all of it…just the really cool stuff" (vs. Dream Job). Moments later, though, Orion knowingly urges Chuck to flash on a lock code panel, claiming without reservation, "I designed that computer in your head, Son."

The testimony of Agent Frost also stops short of giving her husband full credit. During a briefing in Castle during the series finale, Mary Bartowski first states, "Your father originally developed the Intersect as a teaching tool," before going on to imply that others played roles in its creation: "Roark, Hartley, and Stephen split the three pieces so that no one could alter the Intersect without their agreement." In fact, the series will end with Quinn seeking this trio of parts to assemble his own Intersect.

Still, Hartley himself calls the early prototype he downloads "[Orion's] computer program" (vs. Cliffhanger). Moreover, in Season 2 Roark cannot complete an Intersect for Fulcrum without Orion (vs. Dream Job), while Orion succeeds in making it functional without additional help or pieces from the other two (vs. Ring).

The testimony of Dr. Howard Busgang, "the former DARPA scientist who worked on the original Intersect," offers the most clarity on the matter (vs. Lethal Weapon). His code name, Perseus, fits for one working at The Constellation Group and further links him to Orion, whose code name also labels a star formation. "Part of the team that developed [the Intersect's] underlying architecture," Busgang verifies Orion's central role by noting it "was his idea, his vision. Everything is based on his work. He put the team together, he drove the research."

Chuck ultimately benefited from the test subjects that went before his acquisition of the 1.0. In fact, the original prototype was actually created before Chuck's birth. From the files found on the computer Orion leaves her, Ellie determines that on November 21, 1980, "Dad used this program to input a new identity into an operative" in conjunction with a mission (vs. Agent X), enabling the agent's assumption of a "fictitious profile" (vs. Cliffhanger). Unfortunately, the prototype turned out to contain flaws, causing the individual to "become his cover identity" (vs. Agent X). Of course, this agent is ultimately revealed as scientist Hartley Winterbottom, Orion's friend, who transformed into Vladimir Volkoff. "Thirty years" later, after his version of the Intersect is disabled and he reverts back to a "gentle...lamb" of a scientist, Hartley calls himself a "bloody fool" for convincing Orion to help him (vs. Cliffhanger / For more on Volkoff as an Intersect, see Chapter 12: The Grand Illusion).

Orion joined Hartley/Volkoff as an Intersect at some indeterminate point in the past, too. Calling himself "young and stupid," he "tested" a version on himself, perhaps even the 1.0 since it enables him to flash on a Fulcrum agent during the Woodcomb wedding reception (vs. Ring). When asked why he would know to warn Chuck about the danger posed to Bryce Larkin, Orion goes so far as to admit, "I have an Intersect in my head." The debilitating effect of the flash, which leaves him slumped against a wall, foreshadows similar effects Chuck will experience roughly two years after he downloads the 1.0. Since Ellie later notes these effects are linked to the number and "intensity" of the Intersect's flashes (vs. Bullet Train), it is likely Orion took many more years to reach this point than Chuck, since Chuck almost certainly flashes more often and in shorter time spans in his official intelligence capacity.

A flashback scene in "vs. Ring Part II" suggests that a young Chuck, around age nine, may have preceded his father when downloading a less advanced prototype that never causes him to flash prior to his downloading of the 1.0 as an adult. Pointedly wearing a Superman t-shirt, he wanders into his Dad's vacant home computer lab and clicks a button. When his father returns to find a dazed son staring at a screen and "empty files" on the computer, Orion initially shows concern. But when he assures himself Chuck is all right, he marvels at the "complete transfer," elaborating, "You processed an incredible amount of data. But you're OK." When asked by Chuck what that means, a glowing Orion replies, "It means you're special," an affirmation a faltering Chuck will recall to "reboot" himself in the Intersect match with Shaw at the conclusion of Season 3.

Chuck's father isn't the only one to notice Chuck's unique brain. In Season 2, one of the rogue scientists echoes Orion after discovering Chuck has downloaded the Fulcrum-created Intersect and not died, turned into a zombie-like vegetable or become a raving lunatic like the previous test subject, deep cover CIA Agent Jim Yeager (vs. Suburbs). Ironically, the Fulcrum agent informs Chuck, "You have a very special brain. We're going to do everything we can not to damage it," moments before perishing from an unprotected viewing of the images along with several other Fulcrum agents.

Earlier, the treacherous Dr. Zarnow, who "worked on the encoding processes for the Intersect," had already joined the list of Chuck's admirers (vs. Helicopter). After his blind test of the Intersect at the Buy More in the second episode of the series, he confesses, "Your patient is phenomenal. We never imagined this. One person seeing all the Intersect images. All our secrets in one mind." Perseus, when meeting Chuck in Season 2, shares Dr. Zarnow's astonishment: "You're the one they've been talking about, aren't you? I didn't believe it could be true. A human Intersect. Extraordinary" (vs. Lethal Weapon).

Within this context, Orion's gift of the Tron poster to Chuck at age twelve (vs. Lethal Weapon), a few years after his son downloads the prototype, takes on significance beyond a mere pop culture reference. A link to both Chuck's youthful and forthcoming reality, the poster states the inverse of Chuck's and Orion's technical paradigm as Intersects: "Journey now / Into a startling new dimension…/ A world inside / The computer / Where man has never been / Never before now." Of course, in the Bartowskis' case, the computer has uniquely traveled inside the mind of man, not vice versa. By no coincidence, the camera frames Orion with the Tron poster looming behind his right shoulder while he sits on his son's bed, just before placing the map of the Roark Instruments plant in a manner that allows Chuck to match it with the schematics for the new Fulcrum Intersect (vs. Dream Job).

Chuck's seemingly inevitable progress towards the Intersect 1.0 continued during his college years. With his special brain (though some residual effect of downloading the prototype as a child could also conceivably have been a factor), Chuck achieved an unparalleled performance at Stanford in a course emphasizing subliminal image recognition, entitled "Psychology and Symbolism", taught by Professor George Fleming, a CIA recruiting scientist (vs. Alma Mater). When a Fulcrum assassin shows up in the middle of Professor Fleming's current class, he interrupts a lecture on the "subconscious mind" and "how to penetrate" it. Later, viewers learn that Chuck earned a perfect score on the midterm for that class during his tenure at Stanford, even acing the last section: encoded images, with "keywords in his essay responses correlat[ing] to 98% of the subliminal images in the exam." Noting this astounding score, Professor Fleming pursues Chuck as a prime candidate for the CIA's "Omaha Project", a military operation for which Chuck would be ill-suited, causing a concerned Bryce Larkin to intervene with the fabrication of Chuck's cheating scandal. If anything, though, this intervention only delays Chuck's rendezvous with the 1.0.

A few years hence, Bryce, moments from 'death', selects Chuck as the "chose[n]" one to receive a most unique and unexpected email message for reasons that prove logical in retrospect (Pilot). In one regard, Bryce was intimately familiar with Chuck's unique ability to store and access subliminal images in his brain from his Stanford days. Furthermore, Bryce's secret relationship with Orion, perhaps established during the Omaha Project just after leaving Palo Alto, may have alerted him to Chuck's successful downloading of the prototype as a child. Just hours before his death, Bryce reveals, "Your dad knew I protected you at Stanford. I was the only spy he would trust," leading to Chuck's incredulous reply: "I can't believe you've known [who Orion is] this whole time" (vs. Ring). Bryce also held Chuck's moral character in high regard. Early in Season 2, he voices his faith that Chuck will "do the right thing. You always do," in a different context, before bluntly adding, "That's why I sent you the Intersect in the first place" (vs. Break-Up). Consequently, Bryce informs Chuck, "I knew you could handle the Intersect. I knew Sarah would find you" (vs. Ring). But then he adds one final motive that lurks behind his decision: "Most importantly, you deserved to know the truth about your father. He's a hero," a statement implying Bryce's correct belief that Chuck's Intersect path would ultimately lead to a reunion with his estranged parent.

The slew of creative images figuring the advent of Chuck's career as a "skin-covered robot" (vs. Best Friend), sown throughout the first two seasons, underscore the depth and profundity of the alterations the 1.0 forces upon his life. Not surprisingly, a few of these figures cluster themselves in the series' introductory arc. Chuck's baptism as the Intersect, his first flash, pointedly occurs while in the shower upon hearing the news of a traffic delay near the Burbank airport due to security measures (Pilot). Similarly, Chuck leads his handlers splashing through the fountain at the Bonaventure Hotel on the way to his first successful Intersect venture: diffusing the bomb with a porn virus.

These explicit water images are echoed by more subtle ones. The Buy More's flat screens repeatedly project a sub-marine reef world during the pilot and again on another occasion in "vs. Helicopter". Likewise, "Water Lillies", the metaphorical painting representing the espionage pond in which Chuck is suddenly immersed, follows in "vs. Tango" at the auction to lure out La Ciudad. A textured image, it contains additional nuances regarding the resultant inversion of Chuck's formerly sleepy Burbank reality while also foreshadowing a reframing of his view of himself and romantic relationship with Sarah (For a full analysis of the painting and Chuck's initial Intersect reality, see *Unpacking "Chuck"* Chapter 1: Water Lillies).

Reinforcing these baptismal figures, the first two episodes emphasize the pointed selection (by Ellie) and changing of Chuck's clothes for his initial 'dates' with Agent Walker. Equally notable, in both cases, as well as when dressing in a tuxedo for his first mission in "vs. Tango", the frame presents Chuck standing in front of mirrors, his phantom reflection implying the start of his new secret double life (For a detailed analysis of this point, see Chapter 10: Reading the Visual Text Part II). And when not projecting an underwater world, the Buy More flat screens feature monster trucks rampaging over off-road courses in "vs. Helicopter" and "vs. Wookiee", imaging the rough, hazardous road Chuck unexpectedly finds himself negotiating as an intelligence asset.

One more key metaphorical link accenting the Intersect's brave new world in Season 1 is also found at the end of Season 2: the performance of "Mr. Roboto", the Styx hit covered by Jeffster during the delay at the Woodcomb wedding (vs. Ring). Part of a rock opera set in a futuristic prison, recalling Chuck's sudden bondage to the espionage world he cannot escape, the song features The Roboto, a robot model assigned menial jobs in the prison, echoing Chuck's cover job at the Buy More. Moreover, the lyrics, sung by a human who secrets himself inside The Roboto in an effort to escape, speak directly to the bewildering and perilous nature of Chuck's new technological identity:

> You're wondering who I am-machine or mannequin...
> I've got a secret I've been hiding under my skin
> My heart is human, my blood is boiling, my brain I.B.M.
> So if you see me acting strangely, don't be surprised
> I'm just a man who needed someone, and somewhere to hide
> To keep me alive-just keep me alive....

Indeed, Chuck spends much of Season 1 simply trying to survive the severe reconfiguration of his life wrought by the Intersect. On multiple occasions, Chuck is almost abducted by Fulcrum for torture and possible execution (vs. Helicopter & vs. Marlin), narrowly escapes bombs in hotels (Pilot), cars (vs. Helicopter & vs. Sand Worm), and guided missiles (vs. Crown Vic), and is either threatened with being thrown or actually falls off high-rise balconies (vs. Tango & vs. Undercover Lover), a swimming pool saving him and Casey in the latter instance. This is to say nothing of his stalking by an assassin with a crossbow (vs. Alma Mater), his poisoning with a lethal derivative of Pentothal requiring an antidote (vs. Truth), and his facing hailstorms of bullets too many to list, among other perils.

Throughout all of this turmoil, Chuck remains unaware of the top-secret effort underway to build a new Intersect and replace him. Of course, he remains equally ignorant of the fact that upon its completion he will not simply be relieved of his espionage duties and return to civilian life. As early as Beckman's call to Casey at Bryce Larkin's funeral in "vs. Helicopter", and repeated in her private briefing with Casey in "vs. Crown Vic", such an event will actually make Chuck an intelligence liability and, consequently, dictate his elimination. This potential scenario becomes a reality at the outset of Season 2 (vs. First Date), when Beckman and Graham announce the retrieval of The Cypher will enable the completion of the new Intersect computer and bring the close of Operation Bartowski.

The scene that immediately follows Casey receiving his actual assassination directive from General Beckman figures Chuck's ironic situation (vs. First Date). Initially dancing on his bed with joy at the prospect of resuming a normal life, he proceeds to walk into the bathroom and wipe clear a fogged mirror, implying the imminent rediscovery of his civilian identity. However, a moment later, he spots Devon and Ellie in the shower, and though the covering of his eyes and shouting to proclaim his blindness provide a comic moment for viewers, it actually mirrors the more serious matter: Chuck's utter ignorance of the termination order due to that pending return to civilian status. In a separate image, the episode also reprises the introductory arc's imagery of changing clothes, for the camera pointedly focuses on both Chuck and Sarah's preparation for their first real date even as they anticipate the return of Chuck's normal life.

When Fulcrum sabotages the bringing of the new Intersect online (vs. First Date), Chuck unknowingly receives a welcome reprieve from assassination but, in exchange, he also resumes an uncertain and constricted future, both professionally and personally. Indeed, as Chuck begins to ponder the possibility of a long-term rearrangement to his life as the Intersect, the majority of the season devotes itself to developing another chapter of Chuck's existential spy crisis (For more on this crisis, see *Unpacking "Chuck"* Chapters 8 & 10). With a far-away look in his eyes, he enviously tells rock star Tyler Martin, "One night of bravery for an entire life of normalcy: I can't even tell you what I'd give for that" (vs. Third Dimension). Chuck also continues to harbor doubts about his abilities despite his successes. Even at season's end, Chuck will insist, "I'm just Chuck Bartowski, not a hero," to General Beckman before telling Sarah, "You belong out there, saving the world. I'm just not that guy," in the same episode (vs. Ring). Accordingly, that very episode presents Jeffster's cover of "Mr. Roboto", whose plot and lyrics also extend to encompass this Season 2 mindset of Chuck. While attempting his escape from prison, the rock opera's protagonist explains,

> I'm not a hero, I'm not a savior, forget what you know
> I'm just a man whose circumstances went beyond his control
> Beyond my control-we all need control
> I need control – we all need control

In "vs. Lethal Weapon", Chuck takes the risk of tracking down Perseus to scrape together any information he can about the possibility of having the Intersect removed from his brain and calls living with it "a nightmare [that]…is ruining my life." To his disappointment, Perseus calls the proposition "possible" but confesses he lacks the ability to do so and points Chuck to Orion. Chuck becomes so desperate that he secretly makes it his mission, without even Sarah's knowledge, to locate Orion and extract the program from his mind. When he eventually receives the schematics for the new Intersect at the Roark Instruments plant from Orion, the erstwhile Mr. Roboto glues them into a copy of Brian Vaughan's *Ex-Machina* (vs. Predator). Aside from its plot function of allowing Chuck to study the schematics in his room while under constant surveillance, the comic book title foregrounds Chuck's Season 2 goal as well: the protagonist, known as "The Great Machine," voluntarily gives up his super hero status to become an ex-machine.

When they finally meet, and Chuck discovers the real identity of Orion, his father initially fails to "overwrite" Chuck's brain with "a bunch of encoded images that will cancel out the ones you originally uploaded" (vs. Dream Job). However, Orion successfully completes the job while held hostage by Roark, deleting the 1.0 from Chuck's brain during the fake Intersect screening for Fulcrum at the Barstow drive-in theater (vs. Colonel). Finally "free" from the Intersect, Chuck reports, "I feel, I feel different. Lighter." Of course, Chuck's rapture over a "normal life" will not last for even a full episode due to unforeseen circumstances.

The Intersect 2.0, Orion's "baby" and "greatest creation…after [Chuck] and Ellie" (vs. Dream Job), is originally slated for Bryce Larkin, who claims, "This time it's going in my head" (vs. Ring). But before Bryce leaves for the uploading, his brief discussion with Orion at the Woodcomb wedding reception reveals a concern on the part of its designer. After pointedly "reconfigur[ing] the cube" retrieved from Roark Instruments to make it functional, foreshadowing Chuck's imminent psychological alteration in the Intersect room during the following scene, Orion notes "changes to the Intersect, to my initial designs" had been made, adding, "The data architecture is different." When he proceeds to ask Bryce, "What does this new computer do?" he receives only a cryptic answer: "You don't want to know."

Subsequently, moments from death due to the treachery at the Intersect facility, Bryce's last words to Chuck, who seemingly craves only a return to normal life, include a firm admonition (vs. Ring). Fearing that Fulcrum, part of The Ring, "will use this against us," he pleads with Chuck "to destroy the Intersect. It's too powerful. It's too dangerous." Alas, the dire circumstances cause Chuck to place his divorce from the Intersect on hold to "help people" (vs. Pink Slip). Heroically rearranging his view of himself, at last prepared to step voluntarily into the breach in time of need, Chuck finally makes his own choice to download the 2.0 before destroying the Intersect computer (See *Unpacking "Chuck"* Chapter 10: Tug of War). And the 2.0 makes the 1.0 look like child's play.

CHAPTER 2: THE INTERSECT: PART II

The Trials of Dr. Jibb

The online Urban Dictionary defines "jib" as a verb familiar to many skate and snowboarders: maneuvering in a tricky manner, especially when jumping, flipping, or hopping, while showing off. Is it surprising, then, that Chuck accesses The Ring warehouse in "vs. American Hero" by flashing on a soft drink vending machine boldly emblazoned "Dr. Jibb"? Indeed, when the original Intersect 2.0 pointedly pauses beside the machine, framing it for the lens, it signifies more than just a comic allusion to a sound-alike Dr. Pepper knock off, Mr. Pibb.

The new capabilities with which the Intersect 2.0 invests Chuck certainly provide him with many opportunities to jib. While he retains all of the updated CIA & NSA intel data available in the 1.0, his motor and cognitive abilities dramatically expand with the 2.0. With a flash, Dr. Jibb becomes a potentially lethal weapon, suddenly expert in marksmanship and a variety of martial arts, famously including kung fu. Alternatively, he can perform gravity-defying gymnastics, dance, and even give a classical guitar recital. On the more cognitive side of the ledger, Chuck accesses instant fluency in foreign language, surgical procedures, prototype motor cycle operation, and even tying up Morgan! Moreover, his flashes are not limited to visual cues, as audial cues, including voice recognition, also stimulate the Intersect.

However, Dr. Jibb does not simply live happily ever after with this new arsenal of capabilities. Much of Season 3 focuses on the complex interaction between the emotions and the Intersect, the former prohibiting access to the latter if not stable. Unfortunately, Chuck's emotions fluctuate for the first half of the season, largely due to the distance created between the asset and his handler after Chuck reneges on the plan to go off-grid with Sarah in Prague. At the special school General Beckman sets up for him, Chuck subsequently fails to become a "real spy, like Bryce Larkin:

someone in complete control over their feelings." Called "The Lemon" because he doesn't "work", Chuck finds himself sentenced to cheeseball hell outside the CIA (vs. Pink Slip).

But after circumstances place him in situations in which he does flash on occasion and even salvages an impromptu mission (vs. Pink Slip), Operation Bartowski is put back online. Even then, though, Chuck's success largely depends on the degree of strain present in his relationship with Sarah. In a prime example, Chuck cannot flash on his ninja-like gymnastic skills to evade roving lasers protecting a vault until Sarah assures him they will talk about their issues after the mission (vs. Three Words). Meanwhile, the opposite extreme is also evident. General Beckman cautions, "Sarah, I need you to keep Chuck's emotions in check so the Intersect can work. He listens to you, but he's also an unstable element." When asked if she thinks Chuck is dangerous, Beckman replies, "Very. But he's worth the risk. For the last two years, we protected Chuck from the world, but now we have to protect the world from Chuck." Just ask Lester Patel after he ill-advisedly demonstrates Steven Seagal's martial arts technique on Chuck, who is apparently unable to control his flash, at the Buy More (vs. Operation Awesome).

Chuck's short-lived relationship with Hannah, and the emotional release it provides, improves matters for a few episodes, but when he feels compelled to end that relationship, leaving him isolated and alone to face Sarah and Shaw's coupling, the internal turmoil causes his performance to plummet again, leading to his benching. Confronted about his inability to flash by his spy mentors, Chuck surmises,

> Maybe I'm not flashing because I have all these emotions bottled up inside me....I mean, I just broke up with Hannah, I can't talk to my best friend or my sister about anything in my life [including Devon, now]. I'm not a machine! OK, I am a machine, but I'm also a person. (vs. Beard)

When presented with the offer to approach Sarah and Shaw with his feelings issues, Chuck warily replies, "Yeeaahh.., uh, no thanks. I don't think that's going to work for me." Ultimately, the problem is solved when circumstances allow Morgan to join Chuck in his espionage life, providing emotional relief that immediately unblocks his flashes and saves their lives from either the activation of Castle's self-destruct mechanism or execution at the hands of Ring operatives. All in all, yet another line from Styx's "Mr. Roboto" best summarizes this chapter of Chuck's Intersect life: "I'm not a robot without emotions--I'm not what you see."

On the other side of the spectrum, "vs. Tic Tac" shows the dangers of an Intersect with no emotions at all. When Chuck learns of the Laudanol, developed by the U.S. Government to eliminate fear in combat soldiers, he shows visible interest. Asking Sarah, "Could that help me flash?" she replies, "Maybe, but then you wouldn't feel anything, Chuck." Unconcerned, Chuck still pursues the idea: "Right, but I could work perfectly." When protecting Casey's ex-fiancé without back-up warrants Chuck's popping the pill, Casey asserts, "Chuck, it can make you the Intersect you were always supposed to be." Accordingly, a robotic Chuck gives a gang of Ring agents a thorough whupping, but he ultimately stands poised to strangle one to death until his unfeeling gaze meets the pleading one of the just-arrived Sarah, which penetrates his emotions.

This very inability to become unfeeling eventually proves Chuck the superior host for the Intersect, especially after the Gretas of Season 4 betray a similar liability as Chuck when he was on Laudanol. During this period, Chuck is initially portrayed as, at a minimum, falling short of the Intersect's potential and even "obsolete" as he and Sarah begin to take on B-team duties that include extracting a dog (vs. A-Team). Director Bentley elaborates: "We've been studying you…, correcting your father's software for its…various limitations," including Chuck's "emotional sensitivity, his over-reliance on his handlers, [and] his inability to terminate targets." Summing it all up, Bentley claims, "Unlike you, my Intersects aren't afraid to pull the trigger."

At first, Gretas Number 2 and 3, Richard Noble and Victoria Dunwoody, prove Bentley correct, completing their missions in impressive fashion. On a particularly sensitive mission involving a suitcase nuke, the B-Team is assigned as back-up for the new A-Team, giving Chuck and Sarah a front row seat to their expertise. Upon meeting the targets on the airport tarmac, the Gretas succeed in taking out five machine gun-toting guards with only pistols in quick fashion, leaving the bearer of the suitcase alone after he steps off the plane. Viewing the events behind him around a corner with a mirror, implying his retrospective thoughts of the type of Intersect he might have been had he been better able to control his emotions, Chuck becomes one of the A-team's biggest fans. At first

Chuck warns Sarah, "They are outnumbered and outgunned." However, his concern swiftly turns to astonishment as he sees the Gretas viciously and methodically go to work amidst a fire storm of muzzle flashes: "Holy crap! Those two are like Terminators. They just took out five guys in the blink of an eye." It soon becomes apparent, though, an Intersect requires more than just machine-like termination skills.

Indeed, when the Gretas become consumed by predatory instincts that impede their critical thinking, they become "a pair of...trigger happy...evil robots" that almost succeed in incinerating the greater part of Los Angeles. Specifically, Dunwoody shoots the carrier of the suitcase nuke, wired to his heart rate, thus arming the bomb. Chuck, no longer an afterthought in the hangar, is suddenly called upon to clean up the potentially tragic mess, and saves the day with his ability to do something no robot can: "improvise". After unscrewing the detonator, Chuck flashes on the mechanism and realizes that it was modified for use on a submarine, designed to deactivate when coming into contact with salt water in case of a hull breach. From there, he deduces the need to obtain sodium to diffuse the bomb, and after a quick check of the ingredients identifies a handy source, the apple juice Casey gave him. Though astonished at the cognitive marriage of human and computer, mission leader Casey, with the gravity of the situation riding on his shoulders, still seeks assurance: "Chuck, are you about to disarm a nuclear bomb using fruit juice?" When Chuck nods in the affirmative, he trusts Chuck, who proves him right.

In the aftermath, the Gretas, their shared defect clearly evident, are decommissioned. Meanwhile, Beckman, noting that the Intersect works better in the emotionally flexible and critically-thinking Chuck than anyone Bentley recruits, informs the Castle Crew that a search will begin for candidates more like Chuck for future Intersects. In fact, she elevates Chuck from virtually obsolete to the head of the Intersect Project and charges him with a new responsibility: "We need you to find more Chucks." And when it is "deemed too dangerous to put the Intersect into a new recruit" following the lethal security breach in Castle while trying to do just that (vs. Muurder), Beckman communicates the decision for Chuck to "remain the only Intersect." Equally significant, Chuck humbly realizes the value of Casey and Sarah's support, asserting, "It's not just the computer, or the man. The Intersect is...the three of us, working together. That's why it works."

Aside from the delicate dynamic between the Intersect and the emotions, the series also examines the relationship between the Intersect and the psyche. The Gretas' response to the extraction of the Intersect from their brains underscores the burden of its insertion: "What a relief to have that outta my head. That poor bastard Bartowski" (vs. A-Team). In fact, the second half of Season 3 focuses on the looming danger of psychosis, starting with the nightmares Chuck begins having about Shaw, since his former boss is thought dead (vs. Tooth). Ordered to meet with a CIA psychiatrist, Chuck listens as Dr. Leo Dreyfus informs him that his dreams are "a product of your subconscious interacting with the Intersect," adding, "The Intersect is extraordinarily powerful. It has the potential to overwhelm your mind, the end result akin to something much like insanity." Though removed from field duty at least temporarily, Chuck, convinced of the authenticity of his dreams, executes a rogue mission with Morgan to obtain the tooth of Dr. Kowambe at the concert hall. When Chuck's actions initially appear misguided, Dreyfus checks him into a CIA mental health facility.

Ultimately, the premonition regarding Dr. Kowambe and his tooth is verified, but bad news accompanies Chuck's vindication. In an exit therapy session, Dr. Dreyfus leaves Chuck with a stern warning: "The dreams are proof of the stress the Intersect puts on your brain, and it is my belief that that stress with continue and intensify, likely leading to serious mental deterioration.... Time will tell" (vs. Tooth). Orion echoes the doctor's concern with a bit more specificity: "Just like a computer, the Intersect can overheat. Your brain is like a circuit. And when you flash, it releases a surge of electrical energy" that, if unchecked, "can lead to dementia and insanity, maybe even death" (vs. Living Dead). Earlier, the fear of this process caused Orion to leave Echo Park in haste, claiming, "I can't stay here and watch my son die."

The end of Season 3 brings an inter-related problem that complicates matters: the short-circuiting of Chuck's mind when flashing. Much like his father at the Woodcomb wedding, Chuck increasingly experiences painful, faulty flashes that leave him incapacitated. In the season finale, the mission at the Security Summit almost requires aborting because Chuck can't effectively flash, and by the time Shaw appears at the Buy More for the Intersect duel a listless Chuck lies on the cot in Castle, temporarily unable to answer the challenge (For more on this duel, see Chapter 12: Wolf in Sheep's Clothing). Sarah, flashing forty times in two days, later suffers these and other symptoms on the bullet train, too, due to the high "intensity level" of her flashes even though she has the Intersect for a short period of time (vs. Bullet Train).

Thankfully, Orion provides the solution for both of Chuck's brain-related threats: the governor. Orion has already created a wrist watch-looking device for himself that "governs [his] neural network and helps control the power of the Intersect, almost like a pacemaker for the heart" (vs. Living Dead). Moreover, Orion assures Chuck that he can build one to control the 2.0 "based on the schematics of [his] own governor" (vs. Subway). When he succeeds, the relief Chuck experiences is immediate and palpable, both when he initially receives it from his father in the getaway Jeep (vs. Subway) and when Sarah returns it to him at the end of the Intersect duel in the Buy More (vs. Ring Part II). If looking closely, viewers can also observe three governors charging in a case while Chuck dresses in the opening episode of Season 4.

Chuck endures an entirely different type of psychological trial when his mother, with good intentions, takes it upon herself to deactivate the Intersect 2.0 several episodes into Season 4 (vs. First Fight). After tricking Chuck into letting her and Volkoff into Orion's secret base at the old homestead, Frost locates the correct file box and returns to Chuck with both a hand-held device and a cryptic message prior to activating it before Chuck's gaze: "Your father never wanted you to see this. But I know now that he was wrong." With the Intersect disabled, Frost leaves with Volkoff not only knowing her son and Sarah will be able to save themselves with the razor blade she places in Sarah's fingers, but also that Chuck will no longer be able to follow her, allegedly rendering them both more safe. Of course, a now largely defenseless Chuck doesn't quite see it the same way.

In the following episode, Beckman calls the Intersect "suppressed" (vs. Fear of Death). Psy-Ops Agent Rye confirms this assessment, explaining, "The Intersect is an implanted collection of memories. A suppression device hides those memories under what you might call a psychological rock." Before Rye's arrival, Chuck is subjected to a battery of tests by CIA scientists in an effort "to find that rock and remove it," and during this process, the lens presents figures imaging the profound change in Chuck's life without access to the Intersect. Doused with a bucket of water over his face, Chuck actually calls attention to the baptismal image, asking, "What was the point with the water? I'm just wondering." Before and after his soaking, the back of the chair into which Chuck is strapped is also constantly lowered and raised as they complete the tests. This pointed, resurrection-like cycle foreshadows two more realities: Chuck will not only regain life with the Intersect in the future, but, more importantly, he will also rise above its absence to prove himself a formidable spy without it.

When the scientists' orthodox measures fail to stimulate the Intersect, Agent Rye attempts a more "brutal" approach that includes pain and extreme fear therapy, losing his life on the gondola with The Belgian in the process (For more on this process, see *Unpacking "Chuck"* Chapter 14: Phase Three). Not even the diabolical measures of The Belgian and Dr. Mueller in the jungles of Thailand succeed. When "stimulating the hippocampus" as much as possible "without causing permanent damage" still produces no results (vs. Phase Three), Mueller receives permission to "lobotomize" Chuck, that is until the Blonde She-Male and company come bursting through the door. Ironically, however, Chuck regains the Intersect in the very next episode (vs. Leftovers), not through accessing the old, suppressed one, but through the fortunate provision of Orion, even after his death, by downloading it again via the computer he leaves for Ellie.

This reunion with the Intersect proves temporary, though, when Clyde Decker, secretly working for Shaw, again suppresses it using Intersect glasses at the end of Season 4 (vs. Cliffhanger). After firing Chuck from the CIA for his "galactically insubordinate" abduction of Volkoff/Hartley using the Night Hawk in an effort to save Sarah from the Norseman, Decker informs Chuck, "There is one last thing I need from you, some CIA property." Taking out a pair of Intersect glasses, he looks on dispassionately while other agents forcibly disable the Intersect in a process that "only hurts a lot" as Chuck writhes in pain. Thus, Chuck faces his penultimate Intersect tribulation: living without it long term.

Thoroughly human, Chuck evidences withdrawal pains at the opening of Season 5, though he at first attempts to keep them hidden. After Morgan mistakenly downloads the faulty Intersect with the glasses Decker leaves for Chuck in Castle, Chuck can't initially help betraying quiet envy over his buddy's "zooms" (vs. Zoom). Even Morgan's changing the terminology for flashing leaves Chuck feeling passé. But he fools Morgan, who compliments Chuck: "You're--you're amazing. You are so Zen right now. If I had a power like that and I thought it was gone forever, Chuck, I'd be a wreck....But not you, Man." Even near the series' end, Sarah's emergency download of the Intersect creates a momentary awkwardness between husband and wife as they pointedly "chill" on the bullet train (vs. Bullet Train). When Chuck finally breaks the ice, asking, "It's the coolest thing in the world, isn't it?" a relieved Sarah's glowing response underscores Chuck's loss: "The coolest ever....You know, I've been a spy for so long, and I've never felt this powerful in my entire life. It's incredible."

Chuck proves more honest with Ellie than Morgan in "vs. Zoom". In the privacy of an empty Castle, Chuck presses his sister on whether the glasses Morgan used to download the Intersect really had only one reload. Sensing his angst, Ellie gets Chuck to admit the deeper issue and urges him to address it from a new angle:

> **Chuck:** The Intersect opened me up to big dreams. But in order for those dreams to become a reality, I need this business to succeed, and—
>
> **Ellie:** You think [Carmichael Industries] doesn't work if you don't have the Intersect?
>
> **Chuck:** Yeah.
>
> **Ellie:** Chuck, I don't think that Dad wanted you to have the Intersect forever. And besides, you don't need it. The computer didn't make you a hero; it just gave you an opportunity to become one. Now it's up to you. The training wheels are off, you're gonna fall down, but I promise you, you can do this.

Accordingly, Chuck shifts his attention to handling the increasingly difficult Morgansect and directing Carmichael Industries as just a normal—though intellectually talented—guy. All the while, he retains the full support of his new bride to assuage his lingering doubts. Standing in front of the Dream House they can no longer afford (vs. Zoom), Chuck muses, "You and Casey are super spies. Morgan's the Intersect. Who am I? What's my job?" The answer? "Chuck, you're our leader." In the next episode, Sarah sustains her support when joining a surprised Chuck on his morning run (vs. Bearded Bandit):

> **Sarah:** Us spies without the Intersect have to find time to exercise.
>
> **Chuck:** Quick question since you're here. Did you ask me to be Morgan's handler because you were trying to handle me? Because if you don't think I should be in the field, I just need to know that, you know?
>
> **Sarah:** No, I asked you to be Morgan's handler because the job entails bringing out the best in somebody, and what better example for Morgan than you?....You don't need a handler anymore....

In the prior episode, before his mind begins to "melt", Morgan echoes Sarah's assessment: "You are my hero. You're great even without the Intersect" (vs. Zoom).

Chuck proves both Morgan and Sarah right on multiple occasions. Even while he possesses the Intersect in Season 4, Chuck manages to take down Volkoff without a single flash in the climactic episode, using his natural courage and intelligence (vs. Push Mix / See Chapter 13: The Grand Illusion). Similarly, in the very episode where Decker suppresses his Intersect (vs. Cliffhanger), Chuck still goes on to outwit him, using Vivian Volkoff's parachute army and press-ready 'blackmail' to keep Decker at bay and save Sarah. And in Season 5, Chuck defeats Shaw, who retains his Intersect until Chuck shrewdly deletes it with the Omen Virus, for a third time, but for the first time without one of his own (vs. Santa Suit / See Chapter 12: Wolf in Sheep's Clothing).

Ironically, the series structured around Chuck's relationship with the Intersect for five seasons concludes with his growing skepticism over the technological wonder, deeming it something to avoid or even destroy. While on the one hand, Chuck heroically chooses to download the Intersect at the end of Season 2 because of his "special" ability to "help people" with it (vs. Living Dead), he ultimately reaches the conclusion that it poses an even more potent threat to not only himself but to loved ones, and even dreams of a non-violent, family-friendly future with Carmichael Industries. As with other facets of the Intersect, the lyrics of "Mr. Roboto" broadly address this final tension as well: "The problem's plain to see: / Too much technology. / Machines to save our lives. / Machines dehumanize."

When Morgan's cell phone from the Morgansect arc turns up at the Buy More revealing a "stolen Intersect out there somewhere" (vs. Bo), the Bartowskis' hopeful future is placed on hold for "one last mission." Chuck, however, privately expresses concern to Sarah: "It just seems like no matter what, the Intersect keeps finding me. I keep trying to break free, and the very thing that started this keeps hooking us back in." Thus, after Team Bartowski eventually emerges intact from the firefight with Quinn's team at the Vail Buy More, Chuck vigorously urges against pursuing the fleeing Quinn, and thus matters pertaining to the Intersect, before it's too late: "Nothing good can come from it. Let's be done. Can't we just be done? We survived our last mission. Let's leave behind the Intersect and everyone involved with it, and be done."

Of course, the inescapable Intersect, which obeys no time line, mystically finds Chuck and Sarah once more when Quinn abducts Sarah and fiendishly turns her into a double agent without a memory. Even when ironically thinking Quinn dead and a returned Sarah emotionally distant only due to her torturous experience, a sleepless Chuck divulges his new plan while alone with Ellie (vs. Sarah):

> I almost lost my best friend. And now, my wife, and always for the same reason, which is the Intersect....Which is why I keep thinking that I need to destroy it for good this time....Quinn is dead, yes, but there will always be someone who wants it, and we will never be able to move on with our lives until it is gone.

The next morning in Castle, when Chuck reveals his plans to destroy the Intersect while infiltrating the DARPA facility, Casey balks. But Chuck doubles down on his resolve, admitting,

> It is drastic,...but think of all the Intersect is responsible for: my father's death, Volkoff's very existence, Morgan's brain melting, Sarah... Let's just say, it's been more bad than good. When my dad found out I had it, he told me to destroy it, and I wish I had. We'd all be better off.

As circumstances play out, the glasses, now functional with the final piece procured from General Beckman, survive destruction, forming a final set of ironies to close the series. Snatched from Quinn's fresh corpse before he is able to use them, the same Intersect glasses responsible for so much suffering suddenly pivot once more to offer uniquely redemptive opportunities to help others. In one regard, they possess the potential to restore Sarah's memories. Instead, Chuck chooses another path of blessing, again nobly electing to download the Intersect for the greater good and save a concert hall of friends and citizens. But after he does so, and the screen fades to black on that Malibu beach, Chuck still possesses the very paradoxical device he sought to escape and destroy...the Intersect having found him yet again.

CHAPTER 3: BIG MIKE

From Marlin to Mafioso

It looms above his desk, an arched image of shimmering majesty, a fisherman's dream. From its debut in "vs. Tango" to the close of its owner's executive career in Season 3, Big Mike's marlin dominates the Buy More manager's office wall. At least when not chilling in the Wienerlicious freezer, victim of a Buy Moron hijacking (vs. Marlin), or cradled as a dance partner in the arms of a thoroughly jealous and inebriated party-goer (vs. Cougars). On a less comic level, however, the deep-water game fish serves as a multi-faceted, over-arching image that figures the deeper realities dominating Big Mike's initial characterization.

In one regard, the Buy More manager bears every resemblance to a big fish in a decidedly small pond: the dysfunctional big box store he runs, a resemblance that extends beyond his ample physique. From the outset, no doubts remain as to who rules Buy-Moria, and he wields his authority with the delicacy of a hammer. In his first appearance (near the close of the pilot), Big Mike doesn't so much as look at Chuck during their brief exchange when Chuck turns in his assistant manager application, preferring to simply pound his finger upon the stack filling the in-box. And when the head Nerd Herder tries to put his best verbal foot forward, his boss dispassionately interrupts him without taking his eyes off the computer screen: "Save it for the interview. Now go train the new guy." Big Mike doesn't tolerate anything other than immediate compliance either. Despite the fact that Chuck is engaged with helping a customer, his glaring superior butts in to demand, "Now, Chuck!" to expedite his arrival at an interview (vs. Helicopter). Likewise, after assigning Chuck to customer service training, Big Mike brusquely signs off, "Chop-Chop! I got a nap in an hour."

The Burbank Boss also uses his privileged position to pressure and manipulate his charges. As part of the process for selecting his new 'ass man', Big Mike assigns Chuck an unlikely task: fixing all the broken computers on the Nerd Herd docket within two days (vs. Tango). His final words of exhortation? "Show me something." Though Chuck manages to complete the ordeal largely due to the overnight aid of his fellow Nerd Herders, Big Mike confesses, "Two days was meant as an incentive. I didn't think you'd really do it. I'm impressed. And I'm not a man easily impressed." An episode later (vs. Sizzling Shrimp), Big Mike concocts a sales contest with prizes for the winners and severe punishment for the last place finisher: termination, although it turns out he never intended to follow through on either. When the high-sellers try to collect, the deceiver-in-chief reveals, "There are no prizes. And no one's getting fired. The competition was to get you bums to work hard. Looks like it worked." And woe to employees during the holiday season. On consecutive Thanksgivings, Big Mike assigns Nerd Herders to crowd control training (vs. Nemesis) and guard duty (vs. Gravitron), respectively, masking the assignment with lip service to the plight of the "poor bastards" having no family with whom to share the day.

In yet another facet of his Draconian management style, Big Mike reveals a philosophy more in line with Darwin than his future alma mater, the El Segundo School of Finance. During Lester's brief stint as assistant manager, the Buy More boss realizes the Buy Morons won't comply with his hapless ass man's directives because they "don't fear" him and consequently advises Lester to identify the "wounded gazelle" and "pounce" (vs. the Seduction). In considerably more muted fashion, the restored head of Buy-Moria will later still instruct Morgan in the first rule of Big Mike Management: "You can't be afraid to pull the trigger" (vs. Operation Awesome). And when his future stepson manages to reduce a radically rebellious Lester into a state of tearful panic with his temporary termination, Big Mike gives a nod and a wink of approval, praising, "Strong, Morgan. Real strong."

Still, the Buy More's biggest fish serves as a tad more virtuous example of leadership when confronted with inter-pond rivalry. Foreshadowing "The Godfather" imagery that will supersede the marlin imagery in subsequent stages of his development, the boss stands by his crew when the store is allegedly robbed and Emmett struck by the competition over at the Beverly Hills branch (vs. Predator). Heading over in the dark of night, the Buy More don pointedly totes his "fiddle," a baseball bat, in a violin case after vowing to "burn that mother-lovin' store to the ground." Reneging on his no-retaliation policy to exact "payback," he reasons, "They hit one of my men." And when Barclay shows up the next day with his own air-brushed crew, the Burbank Mafioso stands up to him without flinching, resulting in Barclay's ignoble retreat. Alas, the vengeful mission of loyalty ultimately goes awry in more ways than one: not only does Big Mike lead his own hasty retreat in the wake of the comical and unforeseen destruction Emmett wreaks in Beverly Hills, but Emmett fails to repay his loyalty, usurping his boss's rule three episodes later (vs. First Kill).

Big Mike's tenure ruling the waters of the Buy More proves a shallow experience, though, even if it does come with a direct line to C.E.O. and founder Moses Finkelstein (vs. the Ring Part II). Indeed, Big Mike's often dictatorial ways in Seasons 1 & 2 can be linked to a deeper dissatisfaction with his plight in life. As the viewer discovers when Lizzie the Pita Girl breaks apart the marlin to obtain Fulcrum's radio transmitter (vs. the Marlin), the big fish, only a replica bought on eBay for $200, pointedly turns out to be hollow. Just as Chuck repeatedly laments his dead end job at the Buy More, even telling Sarah a promotion to assistant manager means nothing to him, Big Mike gives indications that his gig as a retail head honcho isn't exactly the end of his rainbow either. In an ironic twist, the questions he poses in Chuck's initial interview, "What is it that you want out of life?" and "Where do you see yourself in five years, ten years?" apply to him as much as the candidate.

In this context, the marlin image is stood on its head, with Big Mike increasingly associated with the role of a fisherman looking to hook a real prize, not an artificial one. In a notable image, a trio of fishing rods suddenly appears above the marlin in Season 2 (vs. Seduction), a shift clearly foregrounded in the frame before the camera lens pans down from the wall. A couple of episodes later, Big Mike takes a fishing trip to Lake Havasu followed by other excursions (vs. Cougars). Not coincidentally, Finkelstein's Burbank chief reveals he passionately sought a distinctly different dream in prior decades. After divulging his brief appearance as Rain while touring with Earth, Wind and Fire (vs. Living Dead), he even presents Lester with his prized gold lame jumpsuit to perform in. Referring to another starring turn, Big Mike boasts, "I was a hot piece of meat. A thing women and men wanted," when appearing in a Buy More commercial of the same era (vs. Bearded Bandit). Years later, he still betrays disappointment when not selected to reprise his role in the new commercial (losing out to Awesome) and a passion for managing Jeffster's dubious musical and film-making endeavors. Though his career does not prove "as lucrative as expected" when informed he won't collect his 10% on Lester's rehearsal dinner video flop (vs. Last Details), the erstwhile green shirt still smiles widely when admitting, "Another deal blew up in my face...but I do love the game." Even at series' end, he will still seek any opportunity to fish for his fortune in Vegas (vs. Agent X & Bo).

In the early seasons, Big Mike's misplaced hunger for something more ironically manifests itself in self-defeating behavior, particularly in regards to his diet. Despite his early claim, "My body is my temple" (vs. Sand Worm), he proves addicted to cholesterol. Though already large enough to have worked at The Husky Lad for the More Than Average Man in his younger days, his penchant for "manager only" pastries (vs. Seduction) leads Lester to comment, "We lost Big Mike to donuts years ago" (vs. Ex), a claim no one disputes. Tragicomically, he sees no contradiction in reading an article entitled "Still Lose Weight" while eating a jelly Danish (vs. Marlin).

The Buy More manager further demonstrates a legendary laziness on the job, following the philosophy, "The better my employees, the less I have to work" (vs. Helicopter). When his pleas for Chuck to apply for the assistant manager position fall short in Season 1, the pimp costume notwithstanding (vs. Sandworm), Big Mike tries again in Season 2, freely admitting that he needs someone competent due to his frequent absences (vs. First Date). Even when physically present, he often proves so ignorant of the state of the store that on one occasion he is surprised to find it evacuated (vs. the Marlin). This is not surprising, given that he naps for hours so deeply and loudly that Morgan almost succeeds in nabbing his key card while he snores like a tiger (vs. Role Models). Masters of work-avoidance no less than Lester and Morgan, respectively, pay tribute to Big Mike by calling him "an inspiration to slackers everywhere" and crediting him with making the "dream" of doing as little work as possible "a reality" (vs. Suburbs). The viewer is left with the impression that even his "diddling" Harry Tang's wife is more the product of boredom than anything else (vs. Truth).

The watershed moment for one Michael Tucker occurs when his wife delivers the divorce papers...on Valentine's Day no less (vs. Suburbs). A thoroughly sobered Fisherman Mike pointedly reflects, "The Lady Big Mike is no more....I had the catch of a lifetime, and I let it get away." However, just as the relationship between Fisherman Mike and the marlin figure is reversed, the distressing news soon proves effective in inverting his life for the better. The initial response to his admitted personal failure is to adopt a newfound work ethic, because, as he confesses, if he can keep working, "I won't have time to realize I will spend the rest of my life alone and unloved."

This attitude persists even when he does find love. When presented with "a second chance" as manager after Emmett's offing, Big Mike returns with a new approach after his 12 ½-week stint at the El Segundo School of Finance (vs. Three Words & Aisle of Terror). Bringing the crew to attention, he announces, "Everything's about to change....I am here to do my finest every day," adding, "I do not take that responsibility lightly." When not urging his charges to consider the fact the Japanese language includes no word for 'no', he employs the adage "If you want to sell a house, bake cookies" when breaking out a crock pot station in the store (vs. Fake Name). Even as assistant manager in later seasons, he will stop Lester from exploding an avocado in a microwave with a firmly stated vow: "This place will not fall to seed on my watch" (vs. Bullet Train).

A newfound pursuit of health follows soon thereafter. Viewers find donuts increasingly replaced by egg-white omelets on English muffins offering "160 calories of deliciousness" (vs. Ring Part II), and Slimming Mike reduces his intake to only two Subway foot-longs a day (vs. Bo). His tailor, Clarence, notes Big Mike's weight loss (vs. Final Exam), a commitment that allegedly continues to his final words in the series when pledging to keep "eating fresh" as the new owner of the Buy More, Subway, moves in (vs. Goodbye). Big Mike even begins to count his walking mileage around the store! (vs. Kept Man). The makeover includes new threads, too. The Buy More manager comes to work dressed in a double-breasted jacket following his first date with Bolonia Grimes, a trend that extends itself for the duration of his executive tenure after making an initial splash in his "Sunday finery" when re-introducing himself to the Buy Morons (vs. Three Words).

It is that very relationship with Bolonia, however, that begins the process of ultimately satisfying Big Mike's hunger for a more authentic dream than that associated with the Buy More and the marlin: building a new family. Though the relationship starts with a focus on his sexual exploits, some of them "likely illegal" (vs. Suburbs), it transforms into something more substantial over time. In a moment of transparency with a clearly conflicted Morgan, Fisherman Mike reveals, "I spent the past few months out on the sea, hunting with my bow, looking for my Inner Big Mike. My happiness. I discovered the source of it: your mama" (vs. Cubic Z). He then proceeds to increase Morgan's angst by announcing his desire to make "an honest woman" of Bolonia. But his actions ultimately reveal the larger scope of that new dream: to assume the role of father to a fatherless Morgan. The pursuit of this familial goal subsequently becomes the object of the controlling metaphor that, though hinted at in a prior episode, is explicitly introduced to image Big Mike for the balance of the series: The Godfather.

Only a few episodes removed from his visit to the Beverly Hills Buy More, where he loyally avenges Emmett's injury, the figuring of the Burbank Don is further clarified in the scene involving Morgan's unwitting betrayal of his mother's live-in (vs. First Kill). Convinced that a good word about Emmett from Big Mike will result in his nemesis's transfer out of Burbank, Morgan in turn manipulates his hopeful "dad" to break from protocol and spill on another employee. After all, as Big Mike says, "If you can't trust family, who can you trust?" Unaware of Morgan's recording, the Buy More manager admits that he can take a few days off to go fishing without the store "missing a beat" because of his assistant manager's competency. And when Emmett's devious usurpation of Big Mike's job, enabled by the statement, is revealed, it also leaves Morgan exposed as the stooge, Sicilian style. Lining up the crew, The Godfather, demoted to a lowly green shirt, shuffles his way down the line before parodying the famous lines addressed to Freddo in "The Godfather II". Taking Morgan's face into both hands, he bemoans, "I know it was you… You broke my h..e.a.r.t. You broke my h..e..a..r..t!" And as Morgan drifts off utterly alone, the rest of the Buy Morons, with hostile looks over their shoulders, sympathetically surround Big Mike, who then further extends the parody: "I don't want anything to happen to him as long as his mom and I are datin'."

The meme continues with a scene in the Buy More video room in the next episode (vs. Colonel). While the flat screens in the background post images of Venice and the soundtrack embraces Italian music, Jeff attends the enthroned green shirt while he eats a donut. After Morgan confesses his fault and notes he wanted Big Mike to stop dating his mother, The

Godfather stoically pontificates, "Never take sides against the family again." Hesitantly stepping forward and kneeling, the Godson asks, "What can I do to make it right,...Stepfather?" Big Mike only replies, "We all have to clean up our own messes." The motif is revisited again and even reversed in Season 5 after Jeffster kidnaps Kevin Bacon from the Large Mart (vs. Muurder). When Big Mike is kidnapped in retaliation, Morgan plays the part of the don and negotiates for his release in a Mafia-style meeting in his crowded manager's office to the accompaniment of more mob music. And when Morgan threatens to call the police, he is assured "the police have no jurisdiction here." Completing the motif, Seasons 3 through 5 associate Big Mike with pin-stripe suits, Las Vegas, and Brandy Alexanders (vs. Last Details) as well as a wife with a name recalling an Italian city (Bologna).

Big Mike's transition from the unwanted live-in to father figure is not a quick one, however, and the process evidences an awkward beginning. Just two episodes after he starts dating Bolonia (vs. Beefcake), the would-be Godfather insists on calling his assistant manager "Son," a label over which Morgan balks from the outset. A bit later he tells Morgan that he feels like they're family (vs. Operation Awesome), an assessment his girlfriend's son clearly does not share. And while Morgan actually initiates the goodbye hug when he ill-advisedly quits the Buy More for a few hours over a misunderstanding with Chuck (vs. Other Guy), his conflict remains evident when he returns to beg for his job back. Even though Big Mike has saved his assistant manager's vest and assures him "You can always come home," a comical exchange ensues in which a still-unreceptive Morgan settles for calling him "Dad" over "Poppy".

But Morgan's resistance does eventually dissolve, largely due to Big Mike's persistence, patience and support. Impressively, the former boss takes his dual demotions with class, not requiring Morgan to serve a penance after Emmett's coup (i.e. clean up a mess in the bathroom assigned to the new green shirt) or when Morgan himself is enthroned as the manager of the new Buy More by Beckman in Season 4. In fact, Big Mike shows the grace, enhanced by the desperate fact that he is "between gigs" with a potential fiancé to support, to humble himself and ask Morgan for a job (vs. Cubic Z). And after Morgan reluctantly obliges, the former manager, promising, "I won't let you down...Boss," not only proves a man of his word but succeeds in winning the heart of his girlfriend's son within a single episode to become an actual stepfather.

The most dramatic shift in the dynamic begins when, rather than succumbing to resentment, Big Mike claims he is "bursting with pride, seeing [Morgan] in that suit," admitting, "I never wanted anyone else to wear it. But if it's family, it's OK by me" (vs. Cubic Z). The humility continues when asking Morgan's permission to marry Bolonia and even depositing the ring with him until he is deemed "worthy of [his] mother's love." Big Mike further ingratiates himself by providing key insight and muscle throughout the day's trying events. Faced with a riot he cannot control when the store's allotment of video games does not match the demand, Morgan watches as his new green shirt single-handedly subdues not only a mob through heated rhetoric but also the escaping Hugo Panzer after he grabs Morgan, explaining, "That boy is family."

Morgan manages to lose the engagement ring, but The Godfather passes even that test of patience. "Marriage isn't about a ring," he explains. "It's...a life-long commitment of compassion and understanding. Especially for your spouse's idiot relationships. All is forgiven." With his internal walls stripped away, Morgan proves not only "proud" to give him the "sacred vestment" of the assistant manager's vest, but his blessing to the marriage as well. And when Big Mike responds with a joyful "Son!" and ignores Morgan's handshake, Morgan finds himself returning the hug. Even as they do so, the residue surrounding them from the evening's riot is pointedly swept away.

Ironically, Morgan subtly emulates his predecessor long before his heart changes and they officially become family. Even while setting up his own ass man's office in a Buy More back room closet, and then again later when moving into the store manager's office, The Godson frames a much smaller fish to grace the walls behind him in a manner recalling Big Mike's marlin. Morgan's gesture may suggest his recognition that, as a rookie spy, he is just a small creature in the vast ocean of the CIA. On the other hand, the absence of Big Mike's marlin for the balance of the series implies that though he is no longer the Big Fish in the small pond of the Buy More, Michael Tucker succeeded in landing a much more genuine and substantial prize in the more vast sea of life: family.

30

CHAPTER 4: JEFF

Punching Through

Mention Jeff to a Chuckster, and the smart money says you'll get a grin. It's hard not to. The Nerd Herder's sheer pitifulness has no parallel for the bulk of the series, and that's saying a lot given the Buy Morons he works with. But while Jeff does in fact bring comic relief from the more intense elements of the show, his dysfunction occasionally reaches such pathetic levels that the viewer doesn't know whether to laugh or cry. Indeed, a sober analysis of Jeff's narrative largely reveals it as a tragicomedy, but clearly one with a redemptive final act.

Jeff spends the first four seasons in a very different place than the viewer finds him in Season 5. Frankly, no one would wish to model a life after him during these years. The closer one looks, though, the reasons behind his alternately arrested and bizarre development can be traced back to a decidedly deficient childhood. Events proved to conspire against him from the outset with his premature birth (vs. The Ex), and it only grew worse from there. His parents should have been thrown in prison if one didn't already reside there. Indeed, Jeff's mother calls the Chowchilla State Penitentiary home (vs. Truth), likely the reason Jeff informs his Buy More co-workers that she knows a dude who will torch the store if needed (vs. Cougars). Sadly, Jeff sees an ironic silver lining when he confronts the possibility of his own incarceration: it will provide the chance to see his mom (vs. Zoom). The "only thing my mother taught me from the joint," he claims, was not to rat others out (vs. Fat Lady), though he forgets another shared with Lester: "Knowledge is powder" (vs. Truth).

Unfortunately, Jeff's father doesn't prove much of an upgrade from his mom. When not throwing pineapples at his son (vs. Nemesis), though Jeff claims to have enjoyed the practice, he tried to win back his wife from her affair with Uncle Steve in a manner that ended up turning the relationship into a threesome (vs. Hack Off). Jeff's sister doesn't seem to have fared much better for her upbringing either, appearing at Awesome's bachelor party as an overweight exotic dancer (vs. Broken Heart). Perhaps the worst parental legacy, though, is Jeff's introduction to addictive substances as early as his toddler years, beginning a cycle of abuse that itself becomes an ongoing source of his dysfunctional life.

At Morgan's house party in "vs. Three Words", the Buy Moron claims he has been drinking "jail juice," the flammable concoction that fills the courtyard fountain, since he was in diapers. Alas, his struggle with alcohol is legendary in Buy More circles. Co-workers are informed Jeff is not to be left unsupervised over the holidays (vs. Crown Vic), during which time he blends a high-proof eggnog, and the moment the doors close for the company holiday party, he announces, "Time to get polluted." More typically, he turns to his "best friend Beer" (vs. Cougars), but hosts better have an ample supply. Jeff initially declines Chuck's invitation to share one in the Buy More video room after hours…until the offer is upped to a dozen beers (vs. Tom Sawyer). That's enough to call for breaking out his unique "drinking pants"…and sending him on a bender that requires giving Ellie a card he carries with him the next morning, stating, "My name is Jeff and I'm lost." Jeff even claims to know the dumpster from which a couch-locked Casey needs rescuing, dubiously explaining, "Everyone needs to get their freak on sometimes" (vs. Couch Lock).

However, Jeff progressed to more potent substances early on as well. His mother's lesson "Knowledge is powder" suggests some was lying around the house (vs. Truth). Not surprisingly, viewers find the Nerd Herder "get right" with chloroform on two occasions (vs. Colonel & vs. Beard), and the moment Chuck's bachelor party reaches Vecas State Park he's heading for "the magic fungus up in them there hills" (vs. Agent X). A comment to Chuck in Season 3 even suggests LSD usage (vs. Fake Name). Is it any wonder, then, that it requires several tranq darts to subdue Jeff while only one for Lester when Morgan and Casey need to haul the camping 'outlaws' back to the Buy More? (vs. Suitcase). As the viewer discovers later, accidental carbon monoxide poisoning only adds the exclamation mark to Jeff's problems (vs. Frosted Tips).

Of course, the negative effects of these disadvantages prove plentiful. Where to start? Jeff suffers from delusions, particularly when it comes to his chances of attracting Anna. When Anna overhears Jeff explain he's been "planting seeds" that will later bloom, she replies, "You make me sick" (vs. Hard Salami). Undeterred, he later claims "dibs" on her, only to hear her rejection repeated: "I'm right here you disgusting pig." Still, Jeff tells Morgan that he will take care of Anna after the Mighty Jocks kill him for breaking up their virtual football game, only to be informed that she would rather be "drawn and quartered" (vs. Break-up). Needless to say, all of this would discourage the average crush victim. Not Jeff. The night with Chuck in the video room begins with a montage of his "muse" set to an Air Supply soundtrack (vs. Tom Sawyer), and when Anna returns to Burbank from Hawaii, Jeff, convinced that she will break his heart next (vs. Tooth), is ready to let her know that he doesn't mind "leftovers." With Anna permanently out of the picture, Jeff shifts to hitting on new Nerd Herder Hannah, though willing to desist if Chuck will let him sleep over twice a week (vs. Nacho Sampler).

Though it does not separate him from most of his fellow Buy-Morons, Jeff also grows up to model a poor work ethic. Lester leaves Jeff a bit upset with his revelation that the Nerd Herder spends 3-5 hours a day sleeping in Stall 2 of the employee's bathroom: "Dude, that was our secret" (vs. Seduction). In Season 3, his hideout in the rear of the Buy More appears to have expanded to an office with room enough for at least three to play the new Predator drone 'game' on Orion's computer (vs. Predator). And when it appears the Buy More may be closing, Jeff agonizes over his ability to work anywhere else, implying that his laziness has "institutionalized" him (vs. First Kill). Even when the Buy Morons return with Morgan as the manager of the newly rebuilt store, Jeff begins his first day back playing Leap Frog (vs. Suitcase).

Then there is the, at the very least, socially insensitive if not amoral element of Jeff, who occasionally doesn't seem to recognize basic human decency. When observing Mitt on the verge of ending Morgan's life after Morgan ends their game, Jeff only sees it as an opportunity to "make a fortune" on a "Faces of Death"-type video, and the end of the scene in fact shows him running up with a camera in hand (vs. Break-up). Similarly, no sooner is Big Mike saved from choking on a donut by the Heimlich maneuver than all he can think to ask is, "Any more donuts?" (vs. The Ex). In a different vein, he betrays (along with Lester) no qualms with pretending to be wheelchair-bound in order to defraud sympathetic customers (vs. Zoom), even though he isn't sharp or sober enough to remember his disability should prevent him from climbing a ladder.

The most disturbing effect, however, is an unparalleled perversion that, along with his obsession with stalking, earns him Lester's title "The Picasso of Creepiness" (vs. American Hero). The list of offenses runs so long that one must be selective. Lester reveals the "no touching" policy at the Buy More was instituted mostly for Jeff (vs. Final Exam), and woe to the woman over whom Jeff holds mistletoe, since he is known to use it for "coppin' a feel" (vs. Crown Vic). Even more alarming, 80% of his encounters with women are allegedly without their knowledge, though Chuck also fears for the other 20% (vs. Best Friend). And his concept of showing family affection raises eyebrows when, after observing Anna's passionate kissing of her bad-boy boyfriend on a stakeout, he still thinks they could be siblings.

But Jeff's deviant practices aren't always aimed at the opposite sex. During his interview for assistant manager, conducted by Chuck, he stretches his foot under the table, causing an uncomfortable Chuck to inform him that the action is not welcome (vs. First Date). More bluntly, he offers to "service" a bearded Chuck when he returns to the Buy More looking for cheeseballs (vs. Pink Slip). And in a bizarre comment that stuns even Lester, Jeff claims that Ellie is "his dream come true: exactly like Chuck but with lady parts" (vs. Subway). Then again, Jeff proves equally game for the inanimate object, "ready to pound some plastic" at Devon's CPR training (vs. The Ex), and Lester warns Casey, about to take a bite from the same sandwich, there is no telling where Jeff's mouth has been: "fire hydrants, diseased animals, puppets" (vs. Final Exam). This is not to say Jeff makes no progress in this area. His dubious praise of Emmett's leadership includes noting that under his watch he no longer violates himself on the Buy More property or in the Nerd Herder (vs. First Kill).

Despite these glaring deficiencies, Jeff still provides occasional glimpses that he is not beyond redemption. Just when the viewer is ready to write him off as a hopeless cause, Jeff evidences moments of clarity and genuine insight. Though not the answer to the question he was asking, when Devon asks the rowdy CPR students what's wrong with them, Jeff candidly replies, "I drink too much" (vs. The Ex). Likewise, he is not ignorant of how some loathe him. While demonstrating his alleged ESP ability with Ellie at the Nerd Herd desk, he nails her thoughts about them:

"She hates us. She thinks we're pathetic, and she doesn't believe in ESP" (vs. A-Team). And when it comes to women, Jeff isn't entirely clueless, at least when reading Chuck's relationship with Sarah. On the one hand, he realizes the other love interests in his life don't matter, even when he's estranged from Sarah: "When he's with Sarah, the light in his eye shines brightly" (vs. Fake Name). On the other, he perceives that Chuck must act quickly if he wants his "fro-yo-ho" back (vs. American Hero). Even when it comes to reaching the Kill Screen on Missile Command, he acknowledges, "I can't handle the math" (vs. Tom Sawyer).

Jeff's most profound insight, however, may be a comment he makes about his time spent at Pine Ridge Mental Hospital. It was so dreary, he says, that they put artificial backdrops, likely a sunny sky or flowered meadow, in the windows before acknowledging, "I always knew it was fake" (vs. Kept Man). This comment implies that even in his dreariest hours Jeff knew that the false methods he used to brighten his reality were not to be confused with real satisfaction.

Jeff's moments of insight are occasionally accompanied by a desire to achieve something more in life, a desire that surfaces in sometimes strange ways. Finding the courage to ask Devon for a Jeffster audition to play at his wedding reception, Jeff asks, "Ever had a dream that hasn't come true?" (vs. Best Friend). This explicit statement is mirrored in a subtle metaphor when one ponders the deeper meaning of an otherwise comic trait: Jeff, deaf in one ear, hears a ringing that finds him picking up phones with no one on the other end (vs. Ring Part II). This figure for a latent sense of lack is further echoed when Jeff admits to Lester and a couch-locked Casey, in full Marine dress, that he occasionally wears a uniform to feel official (vs. Couch Lock).

Of course, Jeff seeks to fill the void and gain glory in dubious ways, usually by winning some crazy contest or other. He claims he can eat 45 Twinkies in 3 minutes, and Morgan plans to bring back 90 to see if he will die trying (vs. First Date). Alternatively, he is game for stuffing apples in his mouth to win bets (vs. Beard) when not claiming, "There isn't anything I won't do for $30 and a sandwich…or just a sandwich" (vs. Aisle of Terror). This proves no false boast when he ends up eating a urinal cake that even Morgan only planned to have him touch simply to win a concert ticket (vs. Third Dimension). The same inner desire finds a different expression when Jeff, jealous over Lester's enlightening pain (the result of Chuck's uncontrolled Intersect kick), pleads with Chuck to hit him as hard as he can in a reprise of "Fight Club" (vs. Operation Awesome). Though Chuck shakes his head and walks away, calling them "certifiably disturbed", the lens lingers on Jeff and Lester in the background long enough to show that Jeff succeeds in getting Lester to grant his request.

Truth be known, Jeff does enjoy a moment or two of achievement even prior to Season 5. One, however, goes unrecognized. During his ESP phase, Jeff, charged by Lester to "dig deeper" into the mystical realm, succeeds in identifying who possesses Ellie's missing computer: "CIA" (vs. A-Team), even if the answer doesn't register with Lester ("What the hell kind of name is Seeaa?"). Alternatively, Jeff earns a kiss from Ellie on the lips with both hands to his cheeks when his delicate, behind-the-scenes montage of Chuck and Sarah saves the day at their rehearsal dinner (vs. Last Details). His brief, humble introduction? "Lester never let you see my version. I hope you like it." Of course, his most public success came years prior when crowned the Missile Command World Champion (vs. Tom Sawyer), but the aftermath of that moment links to his present disappointing reality. When asked "What's next?" by the TV reporter, the champion looks at the sizable breasts of the sponsor girls and replies, "How can I make up my mind when I have so many tasty options?" The lens proceeds to morph to 25 years later, when the viewer finds Jeff staring into the Buy More snack machine. Pointedly, he likes the selection Morgan makes for him when he can't decide: Cheesy Snacks.

Thankfully, Devon takes Baby Clara to shop at the Buy More the same day Jeff decides to increase the horsepower of his van by working on it in an enclosed space with the motor running (vs. Frosted Tips). In the evaluation that follows, Devon discovers that Jeff's already polluted mind has been further poisoned by carbon monoxide while he slumbers each night, since the engine noise helps him to sleep. When Jeff receives the prescription it reads very simply: no more sleeping in the van. It works wonders: Jeff breaks through to nothing less than a new reality. Though it occurs several episodes later, Jeff's discovery of Castle proves the symbolic climax of this fact (vs. Kept Man). After recalling the fake backdrops at Pine Ridge, Jeff pointedly picks up a dumb bell, accenting his moronic past, and punches through the false wall with gritted teeth.

The completeness of Jeff's transformation is imaged by the lens when he strides back into the Buy More the day after receiving Devon's prescription. Not only does he look like a new man, groomed, no longer disheveled, and standing tall, but the camera starts at his feet and rises to his face, suggesting he's different from head to toe (vs. Frosted Tips). The lens further implies the completeness of the change by fully circling Jeff while he remains poised in the center. All the while, the surrounding flat screens project images of spring greenery and flowers.

Within this context of rebirth imagery, and the distinctly different future that Jeff does in fact enjoy, apparent throw-away lines from prior episodes beg reconsideration as foreshadowings. Back when Jeff was stuffing apples in his mouth, Lester called him "The Snake" due to his unique ability to unhinge his jaw and shed skin (vs. Beard). Accordingly, Jeff proceeds to both unhinge from his destructive habits and shed his dysfunctional past like an old skin. Similarly, Jeff's creepy question posed to a pregnant Ellie, "Room in that womb for two? Let me know," suggests Jeff's perhaps subconscious desire to start over (vs. Suitcase). Even Jeff's leapfrogging takes on new significance.

Jeff himself summarizes his metamorphosis best: "I'm seeing things clearly for the first time in a long time" (vs. Frosted Tips). This perspective includes hindsight when relating the story of his parents' threesome ("I had a messed up childhood" [vs. Hack Off]) and acknowledging his first sober Christmas Eve ("I'm usually drunk on Manischewitz by now" [vs. Santa Suit]). But the clarity of Jeff's vision of others proves equally impressive. Despite her words to the contrary, he perceives Ellie wants to be home with Clara, adding, "She'll never say it, but it's true" (vs. Business Trip). Alternatively, he correctly guesses Morgan struggle with not having been forgiven for his "dickish behavior" as the Morgansect and encourages him to "right that wrong" (vs. Hack Off). And Jeff is the one who accurately suspects something spyish is going on behind the scenes at the Buy More (vs. Kept Man). Even on the rare occasion that he reverts mildly back into an "underincentivized" Nerd Herder, reluctant to take on the assignment of hunting down the Omen virus, he retains the clarity to admit it's an "immature response" (vs. Santa Suit).

The improved vision translates itself into revised elements of his life, including his moral code. As noted in his advice to Morgan above, getting right no longer means getting high but seeking forgiveness. Likewise, the one who ran up with a video camera to film a "Faces of Death" segment will not participate in the tasering of a Buy Moron, citing "reckless endangerment" (vs. Frosted Tips). No false advertising for Jeff either: on live TV he points out the iPads are overpriced and cheaper on the internet (vs. Santa Suit). And when Chuck twists the results of the Buy More sales conference winner to enable the Viper mission cover, Jeff quells a brewing riot with a newfound work ethic as well, voicing how fortunate the Buy Morons are to even have a job and challenging them to use it as "a wake-up call and vow to work even harder for the next year" (vs. Business Trip). Jeff starts watching his health, too. Alcohol on duty no longer serves as his cup of tea; tea does, served with china no less. Likewise, celebrating the cracking of the Omen virus calls for taking a run, not partying (vs. Santa Suit). And no more Cheesy Snacks; Jeff brings quinoa salad for lunch, suggesting he's going gluten-free (vs. Frosted Tips).

Jeff's dramatic change doesn't take long for others to notice. Chuck confesses confusion over with whom he is speaking during the phone conversation about who will represent the Buy More at the sales conference because he sounds so "normal" (vs. Business Trip). Later, he shows amazement after Jeff's sales conference speech in the Buy More, chuckling, "I don't know what this is, but I like the new work ethic...You keep that up." For his part, Big Mike, shocked to see Jeff reading a book at the Nerd Herd desk, claims he wants to retrieve his camera.

Intriguingly, the precisely chosen title placed in Jeff's hands is none other than *Flowers for Algernon*. Daniel Keyes' novel (released as a movie under the title "Charly") relates the experience of mentally disabled Charlie Gordon, who holds a menial job as the alternative to being institutionalized. Charlie is selected as a candidate for a surgery that artificially enhances his intelligence to the point that he actually becomes smarter than those who used to ridicule him. However, at the height of his intelligence he discovers an error in the research that will render his improvement temporary, and Charlie largely regresses to his former debilitated state by the last chapter. Of course, the story loosely mirrors Jeff's resurrection from hapless dysfunction, rendering his interest in the novel poignant. However, neither Jeff nor the viewer should agonize over the novel's conclusion: Jeff should enjoy a happy ending to his personal narrative...so long as he doesn't sleep in the van.

CHAPTER 5: THE JILL ARC

A Puzzling Opera

Waiting. Whether stopping at a simple traffic light or sweating out the days for the call from your doctor's office on biopsy results, no one likes it. Now imagine not knowing if the wait is ever going to end or knowing exactly what you're waiting for. Ask Chuck. The progression of the Intersect's relationship with Sarah, after a promising start, stalls near the beginning of Season 2, largely due to the fact that he still is the Intersect. Chuck subsequently finds himself open to considering alternatives, especially when a chance to rewrite an embarrassing chapter of his past into a passionate one suddenly presents itself. The Jill arc, the three episodes spanning from "vs. The Ex" to "vs. Gravitron", primarily focuses on Chuck's painful yet educational misadventure in rolling the dice again with his Stanford ex. However, it also deals with significant insights into Chuck and Sarah's relationship as they face an uncertain future. In developing both, the text blends a creative concoction of figures and allusions.

The ill-fated relationship between Chuck and Jill is uniquely framed through the retelling of a classic, an opera in fact. Though Verdi's "La Traviata" serves as the backdrop for only the middle episode of the arc (vs. Fat Lady), elements of the famed tale permeate all three episodes as they reconfigure and reinterpret the tragedy. The opera, set in 18th century Paris, opens with the young nobleman Alfredo admiring Violetta, a socialite recovering from consumption (tuberculosis), from afar. In fact, the first scene informs the audience that Alfredo devotedly came every day to inquire after Violetta's health during her illness even though they had not formally met.

In similar fashion, Chuck remains amorously obsessed with Jill, now a distinguished biochemist, even years after their break up at Stanford. As early as the series pilot, Ellie told her moping brother that the relationship ended "five years ago. You need to move on." Though the introduction of Sarah into his life interrupts this dynamic for a season, Chuck's seemingly interminable status as the Intersect, and thus his inability to date his cover girl friend for real, causes his mind to gravitate back to the woman who broke his heart (vs. Ex). Now six years later, while sitting at the Nerd Herd desk, he still mulls over his failed return to Palo Alto in the months after Jill dumped him to woo her back from below the window of her sorority house. And during this Buy More musing, tunes from the Jill Mix '03 compilation fill Chuck's earbuds. This funk dramatically ironizes the Nerd Herder's assurance to the director of the scientific conference at the Sheraton: having set up the computer system for the event, he claims a "fire wall" is in place moments before his old flame strolls back into his life to scorch it anew. Indeed, when Jill asks how long it has been since they have seen each other, Chuck replies with revealing precision: "Five years, four months." Stating the obvious, Chuck later confesses to Jill, "From the second I saw you, I knew that I hadn't gotten over you yet."

In "La Traviata", Violetta proceeds initially and cynically to reject Alfredo's affections when finally made aware of them by a male acquaintance at a party. However, after further consideration, Violetta tells Alfredo, who is also in attendance, to return to her when a flower she gives him has wilted, implying the next day. Accordingly, their love blossoms from that day onward. By no coincidence, Jill's boss, Guy LaFleur (French for flower), dies the day after the Stanford couple meet again, and only minutes after Chuck and Jill's romance evidences a second blooming when sharing their first passionate kiss in Jill's hotel room (vs. Fat Lady). Of course, they must also first overcome Jill's initial rejection of Chuck the night before (vs. Ex). Just as Chuck awkwardly drives the rented Ferrari to dinner, blaming a "sticky clutch," the Stanford couple at first evidence difficulty reconnecting. In fact, Chuck has to be called to the phone by his handlers after he becomes testy while recalling Jill's jilting of him in college, and even after Chuck succeeds in "kung fu"-ing the "impostor", Jill balks when Jeffster's ill-timed drive-by reveals he's really still working at the Buy More, not the owner of an electronics chain.

However, their love boat quickly, if temporarily, gets back on course. During their conference reunion, Jill admits there were some things she would change about her past, "especially about us" (vs. Ex). Thus, after

Chuck's apology at Jill's hotel door for his dishonesty the evening prior, followed by a transparent admission of his current Buy More status and lingering feelings for her, it is not surprising that Jill, seemingly unaware of Chuck's spy life, unlatches the door and falls for him again (vs. Fat Lady). After Chuck leaves, Jill actually calls her friend on the phone to report her sincere feelings and defend him against the friend's cynicism. Moreover, Jill betrays jealousy over Chuck's cover girlfriend, which Sarah fans when meeting her in fishnet stockings, inquiring of Chuck whether he finds his partner attractive and if his missions are romantic. After overhearing a seemingly sexual, pocket-dialed conversation, Jill even springs into action. Compelled to visit the hotel to observe matters for herself, she ironically finds Chuck and Sarah dripping half-naked in the hotel room, leading to her hurt comment, "I knew it," and immediate exit. Perhaps the most compelling evidence of her authentic feelings for Chuck, though, comes later while submitting to Chuck's lie detector test in Castle (vs. Gravitron). When asked, "Back at Stanford, when we were dating, was that for real? You really liked me? Those were real emotions?" each "yes" response she gives registers as positive.

During this lie detector test, incidentally, another parallel to Verdi's opera appears as well. Violetta, though still in love, breaks off her relationship with Alfredo near the close of the play at the secret insistence of his father so that the scandal does not jeopardize the marriage of Alfredo's sister. Without telling Alfredo the real reasons for her departure, Violetta consequently masks her lingering passion and discourages his further pursuit by returning to a former lover. Enter Jill. When a bewildered Chuck demands, "So you're telling me that for the last six years of my life I've been believing that you betrayed me? Why would you do that?" Jill reveals that she still loved Chuck when she broke up with him at Stanford because it was insisted upon by an advisor to enable her new marriage to Fulcrum (vs. Gravitron). Moreover, she confesses she never slept with Bryce Larkin, explaining that her alleged relationship with Chuck's fraternity brother was the easiest manner to explain away the break-up since Chuck wasn't talking to Bryce, who got him kicked out of school.

The imprint of the "La Traviata" motif extends to figure the interlude during which Chuck and Jill date as well. In Act II of the opera, Violetta and Alfredo leave Paris for the privacy and freedom of a house in the French countryside to pursue their scandalous love, and Chuck fights a similar battle to escape the surveillance of his handlers throughout the arc, though his options are limited. The opening of "vs. Fat Lady" presents the comic mission of the nerdy pair trying to avoid cameras to reach the "rarified air" of the Buy More roof for a "romantic" nocturnal picnic...only to observe another camera focus in on their kiss. This effort is followed by the abortive attempt to escape to a mountain retreat (when Jill is 'taken hostage' by a Fulcrum agent) and a visit to a local resort hotel, only for Chuck to be waylaid by his miffed handlers when walking by a cabana (vs. Graviton).

However, the re-blossoming of Chuck and Jill's romance proves doomed from the start since it is really a phantom relationship based on a fundamental lie, namely Jill's hidden allegiance to Fulcrum. This reality is linked to yet additional scenes of Verdi's opera. In both the opening and closing acts, Violetta stares into a mirror to observe the effects of her losing battle with consumption. Reprising these images, Chuck peers into a mirror with Jill draped over his shoulders while dressing for his mission at the Waldron Hotel (vs. Fat Lady). Using remarkable cinematography, the lens, which never presents the couple in the flesh, initially includes the frame of the mirror before narrowing to only their disembodied, surface reflections, implying both the false and ill-fated nature of their relationship.

Other phantom figures in the arc notably reinforce the mirror image, each foregrounded in scenes displaying Jill's deceit. In the scene in which Jill is 'held hostage' by her Fulcrum accomplice at the opera house, the frame lingers on the statue of a woman hit by Sarah's gun shots to emphasize the shadow it casts on the wall, figuring Jill's shadow self. Likewise, when Jill takes Chuck to the carnival the lens frames the couple with a nearby clown mask in the foreground even as she leads him through the staged sequence involving Leader, foreshadowing the merely surface gestures of her kisses on the Ferris Wheel and effort to 'save' him. A second mirror-laden image, the carnival hall of mirrors scene, brings the mirror image full circle, again imitating the opera's repetition, but with an emphasis on the distorting effect her phantom life has wrought on both the relationship and herself (though it holds implications for Chuck, too).

The most complex figuring of the Nerd Couple's phantom romance, however, is found in the music puzzle scene. After they discover the box in the opera house balcony, Chuck and Jill bring it down to the stage, where they pointedly interrupt a rehearsal for "La Traviata", not a real performance, to open the box together. Inside, they find the puzzle that must be solved by correctly arranging the musical bars to the opera's most famous duet ("Libiamo ne' leiti calici"), sung by Alfredo and Violetta, which also plays in the sound track during the scene. Relying on their instrumental backgrounds, Chuck and Jill, like their romance, make beautiful music together, but it only lasts for a few moments. Indeed, the puzzle must be solved before a timer winds down, implying the countdown to the unmasking of Jill's true identity and treachery, and thus their relationship. Lyrics (translated) from the very duet they piece together further underscore this point:

> And may the brief moment
> Be inebriated with voluptuousness…
> The delight of love is fleeting and quick.
> It's like a flower that blooms and dies
> And we can no longer enjoy it.

Within this context, Jill's Fulcrum code name, Sand Storm takes on added significance: she moves in and out of Chuck's life quickly, blinding him in the process.

At the conclusion of "La Traviata", Violetta finally succumbs to the lethal effects of her consumption, leaving Alfredo heartbroken. In parallel fashion, the slow growth of Jill's infectious allegiance to Fulcrum ultimately consumes her and kills off the romance with Chuck. Initially, as she explains in the house of mirrors that figures her distortion, she was infected by her ambition: Fulcrum "sponsored a leadership seminar. After [graduation], whatever job we wanted, they got us. They made our dreams come true." But when Fulcrum's darker aims began to materialize, she found herself stuck: "When someone controls every part of your life,…you have to do what they say. After a while, I found myself doing things I never thought I would have done, but by then it was too late." Indeed, her entry into a fake existence ends up inverting her moral world. During her lie detector test in Castle, Jill acknowledges a false answer with the explanation, "Telling the truth is new to me." And as Sarah sagely advises Chuck, "I know what you're thinking, that Jill is the same girl you went to Stanford with. Trust me: you can't trust her."

Is it surprising, then, that Jill attends the conference to present a paper on infectious diseases? Specifically, she confides to Chuck that she's "working on a strain of influenza…how the hem agglutinin protein fuses the viral envelope with the vacuole's membrane." In layman's terms, the Fulcrum biochemist is studying the process by which viruses bind to and enter cells of the host, just as Jill's amorous affections effectively compromise Chuck's emotional immune system and enable her to carry out her treachery. Even after Sarah's caution and lesson on how spies manipulate their marks (see below), Chuck, Jill's mark, still finds himself asking, "Do you think when this is all over, we could try again?" Unable to resist her affirmative answer, an emotionally exposed Chuck, after ill-advisedly releasing Jill, is too absorbed with her kiss to note the lie detector's negative response. In an earlier scene, the infection motif is extended when Casey disinfects the table used for Jill's crocodile tears over LaFleur's murder.

Thankfully, Chuck's experience with the infectious Jill enjoys an ending more redeeming than that offered in "La Traviata". Whereas Violetta's death leaves Alfredo devastated, Jill's second betrayal and prison sentence lead to Chuck's final, irrevocable curing from his infatuation with the Stanford nerd queen. Within this context, the scene in which Chuck is injected with the poison at the science conference to make the antidote, saving the attendees, foreshadows his own emotional paradigm at the arc's conclusion. Notably basing his decision not to let his ex get away on the threat she posed to Sarah in the Buy More, Chuck ironically inverts the dynamic of his Stanford days when deviously locking down the one who cast him off in the Nerd Herder: "You're under arrest, Jill, and I'm breaking up with you." Ellie perhaps summarizes it best when talking with Chuck in the last lines of the arc: "You had to go through all that stuff with Jill to figure out who the one is for you. And now that you've found her, you'll stop wondering about somebody else." If nothing else, Chuck learns the lesson of the lyrics from Frightened Rabbit's "Keep Yourself Warm", which accents the passionate scene in his bedroom with Jill, her blouse over the surveillance camera: "You don't know who's in your bed / It takes more than [sleeping with] someone / You don't know to keep warm."

Speaking of beds, Casey need not lose sleep about a mission linked to "another frickin' opera" (vs. Gravitron). There won't be any more; Chuck's rehearsals are over, especially when the one starring Chuck and Jill turns out to be a comic one. Subtly mocking the relationship, the flat screens at the Buy More broadcast "What's Opera, Doc", the Warner Bros.

cartoon classic featuring a dancing Bugs Bunny and Elmer Fudd, during two scenes at the Buy More involving Jill: Chuck's desperate call to her after she sees him half-naked with Sarah in the hotel room and Morgan's later confronting Chuck about not keeping him in the loop about Jill. Thus, the title of Verdi's opera serves as a final link to their contemporary tragicomedy. Translated "The Fallen Woman", "La Traviata" fits Jill to a T given the series' reinterpreted narrative.

While the arc presents Jill as the Fallen Woman, it also links Sarah to a new figure. Up to this point, and also in selected future situations up to Season 3's "vs. American Hero", the series largely presents Agent Walker as a fish out of water (See *Unpacking "Chuck"* Chapter 2: Fish Out of Water & Chapter 4: A Slow and Painful Awakening). But as she increasingly awakens to the depth and nature of her feelings for Chuck, particularly after "vs. Marlin", "vs. First Date" and "vs. Break-Up", her self-defense mechanism for dealing with the separation required by the reinstatement of the handler/asset relationship shifts a bit. When Chuck's dinner date with Jill begins to go sideways due to Chuck's lingering sting over how matters ended between them at Stanford, Sarah calls Chuck to the bar and confronts him over his sabotaging of the mission. In response, Chuck argues, "I'm not like you, Sarah. I can't turn my emotions on and off like some robot" (vs. Ex). Though he immediately apologizes, the comment still provides insight to his perception of his cover girlfriend. The figure just so happens to extend itself soon thereafter when Sarah, again in handler mode, gives instructions to Chuck about how to activate the bug he volunteers to leave in Jill's hotel room: "Click on, click off."

Indeed, Sarah's feelings for Chuck, when clicked on, remain on full display to the viewer throughout the arc, though Chuck is often not able to observe these private glimpses. Even as she listens in to Chuck reconnecting with Jill moments after the dinner date reprimand she delivers, the lens shows the ironic strain in Sarah's features. The pattern repeats itself in later scenes. Over and over again, the frame focuses on Sarah's disconcerted responses to Chuck's amorous advances with Jill: listening to Chuck suggest he could use some mouth-to-mouth CPR practice on the surveillance feed; her longing look at the Castle surveillance screen in response to Casey's comment about her "supercomputer boyfriend trying to browse someone else's network" during the Buy More rooftop picnic (vs. Fat Lady); and her blinking, head-shaking response to Chuck's exit from the Orange Orange after Chuck's guileless and ironic effusion over allegedly being with "someone who knows the real me" and the consequent request for privacy.

To these can be added the subtle cues of Sarah's jealousy. Agent Walker excuses her fishnet escort get-up for a mission by alleging, "The Waldron is notorious for its high-end businessmen and their trysts." Similarly, Casey calls her out at the opera house when she questions Jill's involvement in a "covert government investigation": "You sure you're not just jealous Bartowski's found himself a new piece of asset?" (vs. Fat Lady). Though it certainly also falls within her guardian role as Chuck's handler, one gets the impression that Sarah's veiled threat to Jill after the 'hostage' scene in the opera house, voiced with a tight-lipped stare, is about more than just official business: "It's my job to protect him...from anything." Indeed, she will voice similar sentiments a few episodes later when whispering in his ear before leaving the Buy More with his bracelet dangling around her wrist in "vs. Santa Claus".

In other instances, however, her feelings prove on display right before Chuck's eyes...if he had eyes to see. Take the scene when Chuck returns to the van after placing the bug in Jill's hotel room. With longing eyes a bit wider and head a bit more tilted than usual, Sarah asks, "What happened?" And when Chuck dreamily replies that they "really connected" and adds, without guile, "She kissed me. No spy stuff, no lies. Just me," the conflict in Sarah's features is evident. In fact, when Chuck notes he may have turned the bug off and Sarah replies, "Why would you do that?" the timing of the response and her non-verbal cues leave the impression that she's really inquiring about his romantic reconnection with Jill. Most telling, though, is the scene in which Sarah gives Chuck an impromptu lesson about spies placing their assigned marks under their "spells". In a scene saturated with dramatic irony, Sarah shows Chuck, her personal mark, how Jill will likely "make certain that...you love her" in an "emotionally exposed...intimate moment" with a kiss (vs. Gravitron). By the time she slowly and tenderly completes the lesson, as if she wants the moment to last, Sarah's own voice becomes husky and her eyes, formerly looking longingly on Chuck's closed eyes, also begin to close with passion. And when Chuck leaves, himself still emotionally wobbly, Sarah furtively follows his exit from Castle with her eyes and a troubled expression.

So how does this make Sarah a robot? Despite her sustained feelings for Chuck, Sarah turns them off in her public interaction with him, especially during his relationship with Jill, since it is not only her professional obligation but also a means of protecting herself. The Orange Orange scene serves as Exhibit A for this dynamic (vs. Fat Lady). Moments after sadly telling Casey that Chuck is "entitled to a real [girlfriend]" while watching the feed of the Buy More rooftop picnic, she shifts into robot mode, proclaiming her intention to deal with the incoming "Bogey at 5" with inauthentic bravado. And when Chuck proceeds to assure her that things are "great," Sarah clicks on the mask of a forced, too-broad smile accented with an approving nod and compliments him: "From everything I've seen, she seems like a great girl." Likewise, just when she is succumbing to her feelings while giving Chuck his spy lesson in Castle, her eyes closing and her voice filling with emotion, she pulls back at the last moment and, clicking her feelings off, assures Chuck, "OK, good! You're all set!" before assuming a nonchalant stance and leaving Chuck with blinking eyes.

In this context, the scene in which Sarah and Casey are held in the detention cell by Leader and the treacherous Jill adds intriguing texture that complements the robot figure (vs. Gravitron). Notably omitting Casey, the frame presents a phantom image of Sarah, appearing on the screen of a monitor outside the cell, and the actual Sarah, sitting inside the cell, in the same frame, implying her dual role as spy (screen) and lover (actual) with the added connotation of the invisible barrier (i.e. transparent walls) of her emotional imprisonment thrown in! Thus, when Sarah ends the arc by telling Chuck to remain authentic and, with a wink, "Leave the deception to me," it would seem she is talking about not only her role as a spy but also her turn as a cover girlfriend who ostensibly clicks off her emotions, at least to the outside world.

The other key image in the Jill arc figuring Chuck and Sarah's relationship is the Venetian puzzle box. A puzzled Chuck certainly betrays bouts of confusion and delusion in the midst of his emotional sand storm. On the one hand, Chuck denies there is anything real about his relationship with his cover girlfriend, claiming there's "nothing to be jealous about" and not disputing her question if it's all fake (vs. Ex). And when Jill proceeds to comment that such a dynamic must be "really lonely," Chuck betrays his ignorance: "Yeah, it is. But now that you're here, maybe we can have something real." Later, though, when asked if his cover girlfriend "is pretty" (vs. Fat Lady), Chuck struggles with the answer and ends up rambling: "Um, well I could understand how a typical heterosexual male might find her aesthetically pleasing, you know. And if someone were to ask me, 'Chuck, technically, objectively, do you find your CIA handler Sarah attractive?' Then I might say, 'Technically, objectively, sure.'" And when opening the puzzle box requires them to frantically share the shower to wash each other's half-naked bodies, implying their authentic, essential selves, the slow motion segment clearly ironizes his words: he soon forgets the water is "so, so, so cold!"

For her part, Sarah also evidences puzzlement. In a crucial moment, when Chuck grabs the flash drive with the identity of the Fulcrum agents and flees from Castle to 'save' Jill, the spy in her cannot overcome the lover in her even to 'cap' Chuck, falling back on the excuse that he's the Intersect (For more on the reflection imagery in this scene, see *Unpacking "Chuck"* Chapter 4: Symmetries and Ironies). As the image of the phantom screen/real Sarah in Castle's detention cell discussed above implies, exactly how will they ever be sprung from the handler/asset prison? Sarah has no answers to offer, for when she studies the Venetian puzzle box Chuck brings to her, she pointedly laments, "It's locked." Remarkably, however, she remains supportive of Chuck throughout the arc while letting the puzzle sort itself out. And despite her moments of veiled jealousy, Sarah checks up on him as a friend, helps him prepare for missions, attempts to protect him from assuming missions that he is not emotionally strong enough to withstand, and advocates for his privacy even if it means allowing Jill to put her blouse over the surveillance camera in Chuck's room.

At first glance the music and Venetian puzzles presented in the arc may seem alike. In fact, Chuck does voice the same line when each respective puzzle is opened: "Let's see what we got!" As it turns out, however, the Venetian puzzle box that Chuck opens with Sarah features several elements that distinguish it from the music box puzzle Chuck solves with Jill, and what the viewer ends up seeing are two very different outcomes. First, there is no timer linked to the Venetian box, indicating time is not running out on the Castle Couple's relationship. Also, Chuck and Sarah peer into the Venetian box together. Not only does the camera angle look up at their faces from within the box, but they proceed to stare at each other after doing so, implying their shared interest in the outcome. In contrast, Jill looks on from a distance as Chuck takes the music box out of its trap door hiding place, and then they both stand back as Casey opens the box on the table on stage (vs. Fat Lady).

Third, Chuck solves the Venetian box by using the "complicated" Fibonacci sequence, one in which each number is the sum of the two prior numbers in the chain. In one regard, this suggests that the puzzle of Chuck and Sarah's relationship will ultimately be unlocked by the sum of its preceding stages. This idea is extended when one realizes the Fibonacci sequence, when graphed, creates the famed Golden Spiral associated with the symmetrical growth of natural objects (e. g. shells, pineapples, etc.); thus, it implies that the Jill interlude is merely an educational stage in the larger growth cycle of their relationship. This makes Chuck's early and seemingly ironic statement to Jill about his time at the Buy More cover, "a wonderful, growing experience," a tad less so (vs. Ex).

Finally, a few details associated with the Venetian box foreshadow a rebirth of, and/or change in, Chuck and Sarah's relationship. Not only is the puzzle associated with "Renaissance spies" (i.e. French for "rebirth"), but the opera glasses found inside are linked to the Culper spy ring, which operated during the American Revolution. Aside from the obvious allusion to dramatic political (i.e. romantic) change, the glasses in the Revolution reference also hint at the Castle couple's ultimately enhanced vision of one another. Even the glasses' purpose, "pass[ing] along information," indicates that the events will provide useful data to Chuck and Sarah as they each privately assess their relationship in the aftermath.

By no coincidence, Chuck tells Ellie in the closing moments of the arc, "Jill, Stanford and Bryce, that's a story from my past. But my *new* story is you and Sarah." By the way, the lens notably foregrounds that same sister washing her windows the moment her changed brother, upon learning of Jill's second betrayal of him, walks into the apartment just having accepted the mission to take Jill down. In concert with all of this, then, the shower that Chuck and Sarah take after being sprayed with Rootin' Raspberry punch is more than just a temporal cleansing, but also a sign that their relationship is headed toward dramatic change; they're just trying to figure out "the exact formula."

The Jill arc opens with an ironic nod to *Romeo and Juliet*, which not only images Chuck's failed attempt to woo Jill beneath the window of her Stanford sorority house but foreshadows the results the second time around as well. In contrast, the arc closes with Chuck and Sarah entering the fountain courtyard hand in hand, with Chuck confessing to Sarah,

"I'm glad I have you." His cover girlfriend, about to retake her place beside him at the Thanksgiving table, agrees: "We're better as a team." In a book end figure, the courtyard scene is subtly shot from a second story balcony panning down, reversing the angle of the opening 'balcony' scene. As time will tell, Chuck and Sarah's future will prove the opposite of Chuck and Jill's, for the gift of the bracelet, signaling the change in his cover girlfriend's status to Chuck's real girlfriend, is only three episodes distant (See *Unpacking "Chuck"* Chapter 7: Thunder and Rain). And in many ways, this change will prove the result of a lesson both (re-)learn at Jill's expense: a real relationship with each other is worth the wait.

CHAPTER 6: DEVON

Adam in Marble

Bare-chested, sweat glistening on his shirtless torso, the chiseled six-footer interrupts his work-out to answer the knock on the door...only to find himself answering an improbable question: "Have you ever had a dream that never came true?" (vs. Best Friend). Shifting his chin and pursing his lips, the 21st century Adonis ponders before replying without a hint of irony: "No." In most cases, viewers would smirk at the speaker's self-delusion or shout "Liar!" at the screen. Not this time. While Devon does in fact fall short of flawlessness, there are still plenty of reasons why they call him Captain Awesome.

Much of the series portrays Devon as the nearest thing to a model of human perfection, a status implied by the mention of his stint modeling for Abercrombie & Fitch as a college frat boy (vs. Bearded Bandit). By no coincidence, the adult Mr. Woodcomb assumes the role of Adam on Halloween (accompanied by Ellie as Eve), the pinnacle of creation (vs. Sandworm), though covered by a tad more than just a fig leaf. If those links to the ideal aren't obvious enough, viewers can't miss the 9' marble statue worthy of Michelangelo Premier Goya unveils when honoring his savior at a Costa Grava gala (vs. Coup D'Etat). These images find reinforcement in the Season 2 scene where Devon, searching his suspicious neighbor's apartment, is confronted by the freshly promoted Colonel Casey (vs. Colonel). Troubled by the surveillance photos and monitors as well as security features filling the apartment, Devon ignorantly tries to reach out to the erstwhile green shirt by suggesting there was a time in his own life that he didn't have a lot going on either, namely a "dead end job" and "no girl" (vs. Dream Job). Unable to mask his surprise, Casey asks,

"Really?", but Devon readily reveals the lie, admitting, "Well, no, John," before adding a bit more comedy: "But this is not the answer."

Devon's natural good looks draw the most immediate attention. Woody and Honey's son actually emerged sublime from the womb, if one is to believe his self-congratulating mother: "Devon was amazing right from the start. Really great genes, I guess" (vs. Aisle of Terror). His facial features prove so striking that others freely profess amazement. While Morgan calls him "a freakish bubble of handsomeness" (vs. American Hero), Lester notices the tone and smoothness of his "dulce de leche" skin (vs. Phase III). Of course, the ladies notice, too. Sidney, the fetching but lethal Ring operative, regrets she will have to ruin "that lovely face of yours" if he doesn't follow instructions (vs. Operate Awesome), and later caresses it with pleasure when she isn't forced to.

Adding to this, Devon builds a phenomenal physique. Indeed, Premier Goya proves so impressed with his savior's appearance that, much to Chuck's consternation, he marvels to all present that Chuck isn't "half the man" of his brother-in-law (vs. Angel del Muerte). Ironically, Chuck himself places the exclamation mark on Devon's masculine endowment. Though still recovering from seeing his sister's boyfriend naked in the shower without his fig leaf, he feels compelled to congratulate his Awesomeness on "whatever God gave you there" (vs. First Date). But while genetics may be his friend, Devon largely achieves his enviable frame through an obsession with fitness.

Captain Awesome takes great care with his diet, starting off each day with a ginseng protein shake promoting yang energy for breakfast (vs. Tom Sawyer). Moreover, Devon insists the foul-smelling concoction helps with flushing out the digestive system, claiming, "That is the taste of a healthy colon" (vs. Broken Heart). When eating solid food, the chef is sure to include healthy ingredients: goat cheese, organic nonfat milk, and flaxseed oil for "a real midday kick start," just to name a few (vs. Living Dead). And on the occasion he plans to binge at a Mongolian barbecue, he insists on fasting beforehand. Even tea does not escape his vigilance: he imbibes chamomile because it offers half the caffeine (vs. Tooth).

Devon's marble-like physique isn't entirely the result of diet, though. Captain Awesome complements what he eats by pursuing a rigorous training regimen. Many episodes present him intensely spinning the wheels on his stationary bike in the apartment, so much so that he occasionally won't stop to answer the door to ensure his heart rate remains in the red zone (vs. Angel del Muerte). Other scenes show him performing his best bat imitation, hanging upside down while completing crunches for ab work. Not one to neglect his upper body, Devon boasts of "tri-blasting" his biceps (vs. Coup D'Etat), too, and even develops a faux weight workout beneath the Buy More to fool Jeffster, claiming it makes his "biceps go nuclear" (vs. Kept Man). Is it any surprise, then, that Chuck's cell phone screen pictures Devon kissing them? As for agility, Devon claims he can still run a 4.4 second forty yard dash (vs. Angel del Muerte) and comically informs a snooping Jack Burton he shouldn't try to outrun him, because he possesses "superior form" (vs. Wedding Planner).

Speaking of fitness, Awesome evidences no problems keeping pace with his vigorous libido either. Citing the "wang energy" his ginseng shakes provide (vs. Tom Sawyer), Devon reminisces on his pre-marital adventures in Amsterdam, a "lovely city; lot of canals" (vs. First Date). However, Ellie knows from firsthand experience. The couple misses the first day of rounds in medical school when quickly rounding the bases in a hospital closet and feverishly "gaining an appreciation of the human body" (vs. Angel del Muerte). Even while living in the apartment, Devon always proves ready for a "drive through" (vs. Best Friend), and marriage doesn't slow him down. While visiting Costa Grava as a guest of Premier Goya, Mr. Woodcomb, admitting his wife is causing him to "run a little caliente", steers her off to the nearest empty room (vs. Coup D'Etat).

Captain Awesome, though, is not simply a gorgeous and virile jock. As Sidney succinctly summarizes, Devon proves "talented and cute" (vs. Operation Awesome). A Tony Robbins fan (vs. First Date), Devon shows sustained motivation in achieving his professional success. After nine years of post-graduate education (vs. Angel del Muerte), Devon specializes in cardio-thoracic medicine (vs. Break-up) and is ultimately tapped to head up the cardiac division at a Chicago hospital (vs. Sarah). When exhausted from a sleepless, "tough night" (vs. Best Friend), he admits to Chuck that "saving lives can get pretty gnarly sometimes." However, Devon's formal education extends beyond medicine. He coaches Chuck for his spy conference presentation by telling him to "give equal eye contact to all four quadrants" of the audience (vs. Bearded Bandit), and jaws drop in Castle while viewing the televised press conference in which he confidently engages a reporter speaking fluent Spanish (vs. Angel del Muerte). Even Sarah responds by asking Chuck,

"Is there anything your brother-in-law can't do?" Chuck's answer: "Well, thus the nickname."

But Devon also dispenses noteworthy bits of wisdom to others that can't be learned in a classroom. When Chuck must operate on Casey's wound to prove he is not a spy at the Costa Grava embassy, Devon shrewdly deals with the emergency by calmly encouraging his brother-in-law: "Chuck, you've got the hands of a surgeon, Bro. Don't think about the guns. [Casey's] not your friend; he's your patient" (vs. Angel del Muerte). It works, and Chuck flashes. In another regard, Awesome reveals that he knows more about the realities of life than some viewers might expect. In his relationship with Ellie, he extols not only the view that "partnership is trust" when she balks at the Jeffster wedding reception audition staged in the Buy More (vs. Best Friend), but he has the sober insight to answer Ellie's concern over why their relationship lost its romantic zest after marriage and a child: "Real life happened" (vs. Angel del Muerte). And while Morgan agonizes over losing his Intersect abilities in Season 5, he not only commiserates with him, noting similar feelings while a stay-at-home dad, but sagely advises, "Don't confuse a job with your life" (vs. Frosted Tips).

Devon's excellence expands beyond even having a smart, attractive head on his toned shoulders to include character that in many ways begs emulation. No one should question his courage, for he takes quick, even violent action when needed. Ill-advised or not, his instinct during the Buy More hostage situation drives him to devise a plan to take down their pistol-wielding foe (vs. Santa Claus). Similarly, when Casey, catching Devon snooping around his apartment, pulls out a pistol and screws on a silencer, Awesome displays the cojones to attack rather than freeze and take a bullet (vs. Colonel). During the fracas that follows, he even gets in a punch that earns him back-handed praise from the Colonel: "Not a bad for a frat boy" (vs. Dream Job). In fact, the former football player has a talent for tackling, repeating his maneuver on a disguised Casey to 'save' Goya's life a second time in front of a gala crowd (vs. Angel del Muerte) and again with Shaw, shattering a window in the effort to give Chuck another chance with Sarah (vs. American Hero). Moreover, when Morgan dithers too long to decide a method to take out his CIA shadow in a hospital hallway, Devon takes matters into his own hands and simply clocks him (vs. Cliffhanger).

Devon also shows admirable loyalty, time and again espousing a lifestyle of commitment to others, especially Ellie. Prefacing his marriage proposal, unaware that Ellie sleeps on his lap, the one called Awesome admits, "Sometimes I know life isn't always awesome, but when things get rough, I want to face them together" (vs. Marlin). He proves a man of deeds, though, not just words. When Ellie's father exits without notice yet again, leaving her distraught, Devon, poignantly serving pancakes, is there to assure her: "Well, if it's any consolation, I'm not going anywhere. Ever...no matter how hard things get between us, 'cuz that's what married people do, right?" (vs. Dream Job). Devon earns his father-in-law's praise as a "straight arrow", too (vs. Broken Heart). After telling Ellie, in a phone call from his bachelor party, "How can I be tempted by hamburger when I have steak at home?" he insists the tempting Agent Forrest dismount when ambushed by her seductive routine, simply announcing, "I love my fiancé."

But others receive the gift of his loyalty, too. Devon covers for Chuck's absence with Ellie when his brother-in-law needs him to "be awesome" (vs. Colonel). Telling his despondent sister, "Trust me: he loves you," Awesome later assures Chuck, "I got your back, Bro." A season later, Devon supports both Chuck and Ellie even at the risk of his life by joining with her and Morgan in going after Shaw when Chuck is slated for annihilation (vs. Subway). Likewise, Awesome honors his Hippocratic Oath and refuses to leave the Costa Grava embassy while the life of Premier Goya remains in danger even though the decision places him in jeopardy with trigger-happy lieutenants (vs. Angel del Muerte). On a less dramatic level, he agrees to help Big Mike with cutting a Buy More commercial, linking it to the same reason he's taking time off from work: to help out family (vs. Bearded Bandit).

In a final facet of his chisel-worthy character, the Edenic creation exhibits moments of touching sensitivity with most everyone with whom he comes in contact. Most of these moments, understandably, involve Ellie. Just as he makes pancakes to relieve the sudden departure of her father (vs. Dream Job), Awesome becomes obsessed with purchasing baby products in order to prevent Ellie from "thinking something or someone is missing" in light of her mother's absence during her pregnancy (vs. Suitcase). Devon also concerns himself with her flagging self-esteem.

When Ellie calls herself "just a stay-at-home mom" (vs. Masquerade), he tells her to "stop right there" before reminding her, "You are Eleanor Bartowski Woodcomb, Ph. D, M.D., the brainiest, sexiest, kick-assiest woman I have ever known" (vs. A-Team). And he can't resist a postscript: "You're Mrs. Awesome."

Likewise, when her spirits flag on the Doctors Without Borders mission, he reminds her, "Remember how they said this will be the toughest job you'll ever love? We're making a difference" (vs. Role Models). That and a 'date night' help turn her emotional tide. To this list can be added both his worry over the resumption of Chuck's spying career, claiming that his sister needs to know that the people around her are really there for her with a new child (vs. Suitcase), and the "average day" pampering of his wife: a warm towel waiting for her shower in the morning, followed by whipping up Belgian waffles or omelets and afternoon smoothies with fresh blueberries from the farmer's market (vs. Living Dead). Oh, and one must not forget the "daily foot rub" or drawing the lavender bath in the evening.

Parents and in-laws receive similar treatment. During the wedding planning, Devon does his best to balance Ellie's feelings with those of his parents without offending either, and succeeds in walking the tight rope between them for a good while. But when even his best attempts at appeasing both parties looks like it's going south, he gently suggests "tabl[ing] the wedding talk," but it's too late. Upset about his parents' overreach, Ellie apologetically leaves the table with a sympathetic Devon in close pursuit (vs. Sensei). However, Captain Awesome successfully navigates another mine field when his mother wants to stay at their apartment rather than use the hotel room reserved for her (vs. Aisle of Terror). Privately, he tells Ellie he can bite the bullet and insist Honey stay at the hotel. But when Ellie acquiesces to Honey's desire, Devon first makes certain it's really OK before heading off to make up the guest room himself.

Alternatively, Devon graciously extends his hand to Ellie's delinquent father upon his arrival, even after his fiancé has fled the room and slammed her door (vs. Dream Job). Instead of taking his hand, Stephen pointedly gives Awesome one of his bags, foreshadowing the next hour, during which Devon shares a drink with his future father-in-law while patiently listening to Orion dump his emotional baggage. Devon comes alongside Chuck as well. He demonstrates delicacy when seeking his brother-in-law's permission to marry Ellie, since he represents the "man of the house" (vs. Marlin), and commiserates with Chuck's complicated relationship with Sarah, specifically the alleged difficulty of having to "fake like you're in love with someone for three years…especially with someone like that" (vs. Angel del Muerte).

Devon's heart also goes out to those outside the family. When Alex struggles in the aftermath of her Morgansect rejection (vs. Baby), Awesome becomes her counselor during game night in Castle. Humbly admitting a similar arrogance when first dating Ellie, he assures her, "Trust me: he loves you." Awesome even makes time to reach out to those he and others consider "weird" (vs. Best Friend). Devon grants Jeff's plea for a second chance to audition for their wedding reception, enduring Ellie's disdain and even using it as an opportunity to offer a lesson: "Let a man have his dream, even if it is only for five minutes."

Awesome at times seems flawless, but closer inspection reveals a few hairline cracks in his "marble me," though they don't warrant shooting his head off! (vs. Angel del Muerte). Or, to extend the Edenic metaphor, neither he nor Adam turn out to be perfect. A couple of foibles prove comic in variety. Take Devon's neurotic obsession with Baby Clara. Prior to her birth, he quickly digresses from making reasonable decisions (natural or water birth? Ergo or Baby Bjorn?) to agonizing over Spanish, French or Japanese as a second language (vs. Suitcase). It's not long before he's initially turning down a "babymoon" because they need to prioritize the child's college education (vs. Coup D'Etat).

Awesome displays similar angst over both Ellie's and the baby's health. When Devon questions whether Ellie's lack of rest is due to the baby resting on her spleen, Ellie retorts, "Seriously, you have to relax. The baby is like the size of a walnut." Of course, that leads into another caution from Devon, since the 'walnut' can hear everything being said with ears developing in Week 12. Mr. Woodcomb also worries over his wife's declining the 5-star side impact protection of the mini-van (vs. Phase III) when he isn't bringing her carrots at work, citing the aid of Vitamin A to the fetus's retinal development (vs. Leftovers). He even tells Chuck he needs to find a way to turn Ellie's placenta into vitamin pills! (vs. Push Mix). Not one to neglect Clara's mental health either, Devon is so concerned over the affect the name will have on her future development that it forces Ellie to pretend she prefers Grunka just to make him choose a better one (vs. Gobbler). Later, he leads Baby Yoga classes, boasting Clara "is a way more grounded breather than these other jokers" (vs. Business Trip).

On a somewhat more serious note, Devon struggles with the actual birth of Clara as well. Admitting "terror" (Push Mix), he tries to cope with an extravagantly detailed "awesome plan" on the wall of the apartment. When the Push Mix CD goes missing, though, the melt down begins: "Perfect plan, not perfect" leads to "No Push Mix, no baby." Thankfully, Devon has the number for the CIA to show up and take care of the transportation, but noting Devon's obsession with orderliness at the hospital, Ellie's doctor asks if he's alright. Though Ellie replies he was the same way during his exit exams, she later privately tells her queasy and almost hyperventilating husband to pull himself together: "I need you." Taking a walk for that purpose, he still looks ill, biting his fingernails, while staring through the window of the maternity ward, where Casey, who still regrets missing Alex's birth, gives a stern coaching to his speechless pupil. The lesson takes, and when Devon returns to the room, he finds himself able to silently take Ellie's hand with regained poise. Likewise, when given Clara to hold, he doesn't pull away, but takes their child in wonder, staring and sniffling back his tears until finally finding the right word and the broadest smile to accent it: "Awesome!"

Though Devon gets the hang of being a father, the same can't be said about another narrow crack in the marble: his inability to function in the espionage life. Still, this is hardly a moral strike against Awesome; indeed, his reasoning for ultimately withdrawing from the shadow world proves virtuous. Initially, Devon proves captivated by the seemingly thrilling lifestyle it offers. In fact, the one who has reached the summit of The Matterhorn (vs. Frosted Tips) and planned to propose to Ellie while skydiving (vs. Marlin) betrays an underlying unrest with the mundane nature of professional and married life, admitting, "I could use some real excitement" (vs. Angel del Muerte). When Chuck reminds Devon he is an adventure sports cardiologist, he replies, "I could do that in my sleep...I need some real action, some real adrenaline. I want to feel like I felt on the football field." However, the actuality of the espionage world turns out to be a bit different than he imagines.

Awesome's baptism into the spy world begins a double existence that must be kept hidden from Ellie for both her and Chuck's protection. The moment is figured when, after his fight with Casey, Devon returns to the apartment with the secret of Chuck's real identity and, accordingly, the

58

"mission" to "be awesome" as Ellie's handler (vs. Colonel). Pointedly drawing and drinking a glass of water from the kitchen faucet, he tells his phantom reflection in the window: "Chuck's a spy! Stay cool." Alas, he doesn't. The moment Ellie walks in, he melts down into a state in which he cannot formulate coherent answers to her series of "simple question[s]." Thankfully, she chocks it up to pre-wedding jitters.

His "cover" performance improves little over time. When returning home after his all-night abduction by Sidney, Chuck tells Devon to keep his alibi simple (vs. Operation Awesome). Again choking under pressure, Devon proceeds to tell a ridiculous story about a bear jumping out at him in Griffith Park and having to cut off its head. After confessing, "I'm a terrible liar," Chuck bails him out with the story of a drunk Casey, which Devon proceeds to almost ruin with his exaggerations as well. Later, when forced on the mission to 'kill' Shaw for Sidney, another un-awesome melt down follows. Stopped by a sympathetic security guard in the foyer, it doesn't take long before Awesome is telling him he's "involved in something really messed up," explaining, "I've been lying to my wife… to everybody. I can't take it anymore." Again, Chuck bails him out, this time with a tranq gun. And when a "freaking out" Devon meets him in the Buy More to find out what he's supposed to tell Ellie about finding the airline tickets to Chuck's Paris mission, he gets an uneasy front row seat to a professional liar when Ellie shows up unexpectedly. Stunned by Chuck's smooth, impromptu tale of a Buy More business trip and his plans to send them on a surprise second honeymoon in Paris, Devon comments, "That was so cold-blooded. How could you just lie to her like that?" (vs. Nacho Sampler).

Ultimately, Devon wants to opt out of the double life, and not just because of the lying. Following the close calls surrounding the series of events at the Costa Grava embassy (vs. Angel del Muerte), Devon comes to the conclusion, "I think I've scratched my espionage itch," elaborating, "Black tie dinners and embassy extractions are killer, but…having a double life means having to give up half of your real life." Unfortunately, leaving the spy life isn't that simple. In the very next episode Devon is abducted by Sidney and dangled off the edge of one high rise building before he must penetrate the security of another in order to 'kill' Shaw and keep his head from being blown off by the explosive earpiece (vs. Operation Awesome).

In fact, Devon's life remains dramatically inverted by the danger that continues to stalk him, and thus Ellie, even after his exit from active spy duty and self-imposed state of ignorance regarding Chuck's affairs, a reality pointedly imaged by his performing crunches while hanging upside down during this arc (vs. Fake Name). Continuing to exhibit "really jittery" behavior (vs. Nacho Sampler), Devon is told by Ellie that he has not "been acting like [him]self." Instead, he lies around the house, claiming he has pulled a hamstring, either watching TV or reading an article on kidney failure even as he is having difficulty filtering the dangers of the double life. Turning down the free trip to Paris offered by Chuck, citing the alleged "strings attached," he suddenly asserts himself as head of the household and comically forbids them to go. However, he does plan a local vacation to get away and fix things with Ellie (vs. Beard). Ironically, even that defensive tactic backfires as he becomes a decoy used by the Ring to leave Chuck and Shaw's base defenseless.

This last event convinces Devon to take Ellie somewhere much further away: Africa. Indeed, his sudden interest in Doctors Without Borders really stems from his desire to protect them from the tentacles of the spy life. His emotional baggage at this point is so heavy that it is figured by the dumbbells he intends to pack in his luggage (vs. Honeymooners). Pointedly, Ellie removes them, vowing, "They're not coming with us to Africa," a bit of dramatic irony given that Justin mysteriously shows up there to ensure they return to America. Thus, after Justin causes Devon to become ill with malaria-like symptoms, Devon is left with two insights, one of them not entirely true. Claiming, "You can die just as easily from a mosquito in Africa as a spy in Burbank" (vs. Tooth), he asserts, "Fear is the mind-killer. Can't live scared, Bro. Not for yourself, not for anyone."

Still, he remains resolved to keep himself divorced from the double life. In Season 4, he turns over Orion's computer to Chuck with a demand: "I don't want this spy stuff near Ellie ever again" (vs. Leftovers). Though he acquiesces to Ellie's desire to work with the data on Orion's computer (vs. Muurder), conflicted but seeing how much the work means to her, he clearly prefers pretending instead. A Season 5 game night in Castle with Devon and Alex provides the opportunity to play spy vs. spy with Ellie (vs. Baby), a narrative that makes both run a little caliente. Likewise, a typical dinner date turns into a torrid faux mission with secret signals and code words (Operation Eagle)…that is until it accidentally turns into a real one (vs. Curse).

Of the cracks in Awesome's metaphorical Marble Me, perhaps the only ones that prove egregious are those betraying an occasional selfishness. In each instance, however, Devon remains open to correction and ends up making amends that end up increasing his awesomeness. At the end of Season 1, the Edenic couple's idyllic relationship hits a bump when making a decision between purchasing a washer and dryer preferred by Devon or a flat screen TV eyed by Ellie for their dating anniversary (vs. Undercover Lover). After a retail therapy session with Morgan in which they voice their respective rationales, Ellie, paged by the hospital, leaves with a final directive: "Why don't you just surprise me, OK?" Before Ellie arrives home, Devon claims "no worries" about Ellie's response to his selection of the washer and dryer, which have already been delivered. When Ellie walks through the door, though, it turns out he may have some after all.

"Your getting what you want isn't a surprise," laments Ellie, adding, "It's always about what you want…It's not just about a washer and dryer: it's about what it represents." In the therapy session that follows, Morgan gets Ellie to further reveal she's "banking on my future with a giant, muscly child, and I can't do it anymore" before she exits stage right. After an abbreviated night of strip poker with the Buy Morons, Devon returns the next morning to find a hung over Ellie giving a friendly hug of relief to Morgan in their bedroom. But no worries; in an awesome display of confidence in Ellie's fidelity and a chastened attitude, Awesome spills his own revelation: "You were right: I was being selfish. I got a glimpse of what my life would be like without you: not a pretty picture." Somehow, the flat screen to which he guides her is already installed.

Devon's selfishness surfaces again a season later, this time in his failure to act (vs. Best Friend). Overwhelmed by her "To Do" list in planning the wedding, Ellie vents, "There aren't enough hours in the day for me to do everything myself….I need you to start pulling your weight around here." Tearing her list in half, she gives Devon the responsibility for the flowers, the music, and the cake. Devon initially responds with awesomeness: "A marriage is a partnership; a wedding should be, too." However, citing his "busy" schedule, he proceeds to "outsource" his task of procuring a band for the wedding to Chuck. This, of course, results in the Jeffster audition that never materializes when Lester panics. What does materialize, though, is Ellie's frustration with her fiancé until the episode's end. After the lens follows a large box carted out of the Buy More by a customer, foreshadowing the removal of the couple's emotional baggage, Devon enters the Buy More with Ellie ready to rectify the delegation of his duties. Affirming to his fiancé, "An apology is just words if not followed up by actions," Awesome subsequently informs her that he's not only arranged for the flowers and cake but also her half of the "To Do" list as well.

In Season 3, Devon's selfishness pops up yet again, though, in his defense, his actions partially root themselves in his concern for their safety as a couple given his double life. When Ellie receives the news she has been awarded the USC neurology fellowship, it begins a battle between following that path and leaving for Africa with Doctors Without Borders (vs. Tic Tac). To persuade each other, they appeal to Morgan, who proves no help when he switches sides in a matter of minutes, depending on who speaks to him last. By the end of the episode, Ellie reveals an epiphany to Chuck, who wonders at her willingness to "sacrifice" her "dream since being a kid" and join Devon in the African venture: "...Dreams change. And if there is one thing that I know for sure, it's that I want to be with Devon....He's the best choice I ever made."

Before he becomes aware of Ellie's decision, Awesome has an epiphany of his own to share. "Stealing" her into the apartment, he shows her a "Congratulations" banner and begins speaking even as he hands her a glass of champagne: "Babe, I realize that I didn't congratulate you for getting the fellowship. And that was only my first mistake....If this is important to you, then it is important to me....Take the job. We'll make it work. Together."

Marble repair references will tell you that hairline cracks are usually stable, do not grow larger, and rarely cause problems except for the irritation of their existence. One can fill even larger cracks before re-finishing and polishing the surface to render them nearly invisible. The same holds true for the Marble Me. By learning from his relatively minor missteps, Captain Awesome actually succeeds in adding luster to his Edenic image.

CHAPTER 7: GENERAL BECKMAN

Atlas Un-shrugged

Chuck indulging himself in a Brian Vaughan graphic novel. The camera panning the volumes sitting on a shelf in Shaw's loft. Even a new-and-improved Jeff giving rapt attention to *Flowers for Algernon* at the Nerd Herd desk. Throughout "Chuck", books and their titles are strategically inserted to highlight key traits of the characters reading them. General Diane Beckman proves no exception to this motif. A bit of scrutiny reveals that a seemingly superficial punch line dropped in Season 3, which notes the NSA officer owns a copy of *Atlas Shrugged* (vs. Other Guy), actually implies something profound. A modern day Atlas, Beckman shoulders the titanic burden of preventing a violent globe from falling to pieces on a daily basis. As she states in her final farewell to the Castle Crew, "If you ever want to save the world again…you know where to find me" (vs. Goodbye). Further accenting the point, at least a pair of globes are occasionally visible decorating the shelves behind her D.C. desk.

While attempting to keep an exceedingly dangerous planet poised on her shoulders, Beckman inhabits an alternate world in which a gravely serious end, national security, justifies the oftentimes morally ambiguous means to achieve it. Not only to survive but succeed in this shadowy realm, she maintains a notable professional detachment from the people and events surrounding her for much of the series. This dynamic is figured by another object pointedly occupying the shelf behind her: the bird of prey statue looming over her right shoulder in most episodes. On the surface level, it stares out over Beckman's D.C. office from its roost, removed and stoic, imitating the general when she peers from her remote location into Castle from the flat screen perched on the wall.

Without much imagination, especially given the series' obsession with pop culture allusions, the viewer can further link the decoration to Dashiell Hammett's Maltese Falcon, the titular statue in the famed hard-boiled mystery featuring a detective who, like others in the distinct genre, is rendered emotionally cynical due to the constant cycle of violence he encounters. Accordingly, Beckman explicitly voices emotional skepticism in multiple episodes, including one in which a desperate Chuck convinces Casey to fake his death to draw out Frost's former associates and thus help him locate her (vs. Couch Lock). Mistaking Chuck's self-serving naiveté for the detached, professionally objective manner she models, Beckman lauds the plan, claiming, "You've really progressed as a spy. You've put duty above emotion...Good tactical thinking." The ethos manifests itself even more obviously in a prior scene when the general, while investigating Sarah for the 49B, tells Chuck, "I want facts. I don't care about your feelings" (vs. Broken Heart).

It raises no eyebrows, then, that Beckman doesn't display a bleeding heart while instructing her spies to exploit even private personal relationships when the greater good of the country is at stake. Seeing an opportunity to use Sarah's familiarity with high school nemesis Heather Chandler as an espionage gift, Beckman calls for a double date that creates significant angst within Agent Walker, given that the mission will force her to revisit her problematic adolescence (vs. Cougars). In the exchange that follows, though, Beckman cynically bulldozes right over Sarah's rarely revealed feelings, even inserting sarcasm as an exclamation point:

> **Sarah:** General, I apologize, but I'm afraid I must recuse myself from this mission. My cover has been compromised.
>
> **Beckman:** Agent Walker, you have preexisting social history with the target. Seems to me like you have the perfect cover.
>
> **Sarah:** But it's not a cover, Ma'am. It's me.
>
> **Beckman:** Well, I hope you enjoy Italian food. Buon appetito!

In an even more egregious example, the NSA commander uses Chuck's "social connection" with his life-long friend, Morgan, and Morgan's erstwhile girlfriend to create, emotionally speaking, "a big problem" for Chuck (vs. Best Friend). Dispassionately, she orders his attendance at a party thrown by Morgan's romantic rival that may—and ultimately in fact does—put his relationship at risk as a seeming "Judas" when a stalking Morgan spies him through binoculars. Even family is fair game. When Chuck asks Beckman to confirm she is asking him to "exploit my sister and/or brother-in-law to acquire confidential medical records for government use" in order to clarify Premier Goya's health condition, she bluntly replies, "Yes, Chuck. That's exactly what I'm asking" (vs. Angel del Muerte).

In a similar regard, the general evidences a certain degree of tone-deafness when underlings suffer emotional trauma over potential loss. After Roark seizes Orion and takes him to an undisclosed location for possible torture or execution, Chuck remains beside himself with anxiety (vs. First Kill). With good intentions, Beckman, perhaps a bit patronizingly, explains that the agency is doing everything it can to find him before claiming, "I understand your disappointment." Stung both by her relatively nonchalant attitude and decided inability to relate, given her lack of experience with family endangerment, he shoots back, "Do you?!" Likewise, Sarah betrays unprecedented despair over Chuck's welfare after he is taken by The Belgian in Season 4 (vs. Phase III). Though again well-meaning, Beckman exposes a seeming ignorance to the intensity of her agent's inner turmoil when urging Sarah to "go home and get some sleep." And when the general proceeds to conflate the object of Sarah's panic with assurance of the CIA's own self-interest in nabbing The Belgian before he sells the Intersect's secrets, it pushes Sarah to the brink of insubordination when she shouts, "Forget the secrets! This is about Chuck!"

Beckman's emotional detachment and cynicism expresses itself perhaps most vividly in cases that push the envelope on moral ambiguity. As silently implied by the long talons of the statue lurking above her shoulder, the general is not one to shy away from the most extreme violence, even if it involves members of her own team. On the surface, the question Chuck poses during his first briefing with Beckman and Graham while an espionage rookie seems naïve: "Are they with us?" (vs. Wookiee). Over time, though, the answer to the question proves more complex: yes...and no. Within the NSA-CIA economy the answer becomes a matter of status: whether one is an asset or a liability to the nation. Thus, when the successful beta version indicates the new Intersect appears ready to come online, Beckman prepares Casey for the pending hit order on the current Intersect, who will become obsolete and even a threat if corrupted or tortured, without betraying any outward qualms. Not only does she voice her hope that Casey has "not grown too fond of the subject" but ironically proceeds to sign off, "Oh, and John, Happy Holidays" (vs. Crown Vic).

The dynamic repeats itself with little variation three episodes later. Graham does most of the dirty work during the briefing, telling Chuck the technical truth: when "Operation Bartowski officially comes to an end you'll be done with us. No more briefings, no more missions, no more spies. Enjoy the rest of your life, Chuck" (vs. First Date). No mention of the elimination detail. Meanwhile, Beckman mutely stares into the lens, a pleasant expression plastered on her face. And when Beckman officially assigns Casey the hit order near the end of the episode, she doesn't even tolerate the usually steel-plated spy's momentary sigh of regret. Leaning towards the camera, she presses, "What was that, Casey?" Given these scenarios, it surprises no one when Beckman places an assassination order on Sarah's father, Jack Burton (vs. DeLorean), or stoically accepts Shaw's offer to sacrifice himself to take out The Ring leadership without much more than pursed lips while bestowing him the honorary label of "American Hero" (vs. American Hero).

When it comes to the morally ambiguous topic of deception, the pseudo Maltese Falcon images another facet of Beckman's hard-boiled cynicism. Intriguingly, the mute ornament is rarely displayed in full throughout the series (vs. Imported Hard Salami an exception), either partially hidden by shadows or the head cut off by the frame of the lens. Similarly, the shadowy NSA chief often plays with the truth, either passively hiding information or actively lying to achieve desired objectives beyond her agents' espionage framework. To be fair, she has no illusions about the veracity of others either. After interrogating Casey on his assessment of Chuck and Sarah's relationship for the 49B, she still insists he send everything he has on them, including video surveillance footage. When Casey questions, "Don't you trust me?" Beckman adamantly admits, "I don't trust anybody" (vs. Predator).

Beckman plays no favorites with those from whom she hides information. After Casey's emotions get the best of him upon discovering his former sensei, Ty Bennett, has gone rogue, the general not only benches him but reveals she knew he was a traitor long before Casey did: "This is why I didn't tell you about Bennett: I knew you would make it into a vendetta" (vs. Sensei). Sarah takes her turn, too. Though she notifies Beckman of her desire to infiltrate Volkoff's organization to take him down and bring Frost back, Beckman doesn't return the favor. Both Sarah and Chuck are shocked to find Sarah arrested for treason after a mission the general engineers as the pretext for pursuing her subsequent Volkoff mission (vs. Balcony). Of course, Chuck falls victim, too. In an effort to bring him back to work for the CIA at the beginning of Season 4, Beckman secretly blackballs the thoroughly confused Chuck in the local tech community so that he receives no job offers despite his qualifications and his interviewers' initial interest.

The most explicit example proves Beckman's withholding the information from Chuck about Sarah's real status during the 49B investigation. When ambushed with the news of Sarah's reassignment and the installation of Agent Forrest as his new handler, Chuck immediately calls Beckman out: "I was under the impression that Agent Forrest was here just to evaluate Sarah. You lied to me!" With typical detachment, the general calmly replies, "We disclosed everything that was pertinent to you. That's the way the National Security Agency operates" (vs. Broken Heart).

However, Beckman actively lies, or orders her agents to do so, perhaps more often than simply obscuring information. Too many examples fill the series to discuss in total, but three specific episodes more than suffice to illustrate, including the events surrounding the burning of asset Vivian Volkoff (vs. First Bank of Evil). After agreeing to set up a meeting between Vivian and her father in exchange for help in heisting the bank in Macau, Beckman later reneges, dubiously claiming, "We have decided the security risks are too great." Chuck protests, only to receive a lesson and ironic praise from the cynic-in-chief: "Agent Bartowski, you told your asset what she needed to hear. That's what a spy does. Well done." In burning Chuck to burn Vivian, Beckman praises herself as well.

Similarly, Beckman directs Sarah to lie to Chuck's face to avoid "a fight" when she deems it time to bunker him (vs. First Kill). While explaining to Sarah the reasoning behind her order—to tell Chuck The Ring transport was intercepted and Orion is safe—the general minces no words: "Chuck trusts you, Sarah. He believes you would never betray him. Use that." Speaking of Orion, Beckman also appears to lie repeatedly to

Chuck about her lack of knowledge regarding the ultra-secret Intersect guru over multiple episodes (vs. Lethal Weapon), a point she concedes privately to Sarah and Casey after Chuck makes contact with Orion (vs. Predator). Accordingly, the questions with which she peppers Chuck ("What did he say? Where's the computer going?") indicate as much a concern over whether Chuck will become aware of her lie (and perhaps his identity as his father, too) as the intel on Orion. Is it any wonder, then, when Team Bartowski returns the favor? With the identity of Agent X discovered, along with the cover-up that kept it hidden, Casey calls Team Bartowski into an interrogation room, the surveillance camera disengaged, and calls for the information to remain secret from everyone, even Beckman, at the risk of their lives (vs. Agent X).

In a final facet of her cynical approach to the morally ambiguous situations permeating her alternate espionage world, the general finds herself capable of overlooking certain indiscretions and breaches in protocol…when it benefits the NSA. Though clearly suspicious about how a Thai diplomat ended up in a Los Angeles hospital with no memory of the last 48 hours, during which time Casey and Sarah secretly abducted him from the Thai embassy to Castle and Sarah broke Geneva Convention regulations, she accepts their denial with nothing more than knotted eyebrows (vs. Phase Three). After all, The Belgian is in custody and the Intersect, though not functioning, safe again. And when the Castle Crew conducts a successful rogue operation that bags Iranian bomb makers, stemming from Chuck's prior fake flash on their wedding planner, Beckman initially berates them only to later acknowledge that her superiors were pleased with the result: obtaining the Zephyr. Though she expresses curiosity regarding how they pulled the mission off without CIA funds, she pointedly chooses to hide behind plausible deniability, noting, "The less I know the better" (vs. Wedding Planner).

Ironically, the higher the stakes, the more the general is willing to lower her standard. After banishing Casey from the NSA with steely will for his treasonous actions in "vs. Tic Tac", his reinstatement proves a topic open to a very brief and readily agreeable negotiation. The moment Casey contacts her from Paris and holds The Ring Director to the laptop screen, she deals: "What do you want for him?" (vs. Other Guy). During the inter-agency conspiracy orchestrated by Decker, Beckman also personally supervises Casey's preparation to interrogate Agent Cunnings with the latter's clearly illegal electrical shocking device called "The

Toy". Minutes after claiming, "I'm very excited to see how it works," Beckman marches out from the room, happy to announce Cunnings' confession and the dropping of all charges. In likely Beckman's most ironic turn, she reverses the banishment of Agent Walker and reinstates her as Chuck's handler after her prior decision to banish Sarah almost cost her the Intersect. Acknowledging Chuck's claim that Sarah's feelings saved his life, Beckman ends up abandoning her policy of enforced detachment: "Agent Forrest diagnosed your emotional connection as a liability. But I suppose it can also be an asset to…well, the asset" (vs. Broken Heart).

Though Beckman oftentimes resembles a hard-boiled robot, especially during Season 1, she shows increasing signs of joining the human race as the series progresses. Early in Season 2, the Castle Crew has its collective eyebrows raised when observing a glimpse of the general's school girl demeanor when Agent Roan Montgomery appears for a briefing (vs. Seduction). Watching Beckman blush and pointedly pull a stray strand of hair behind an ear from her tightly wound bun, they share a startled expression as Montgomery proceeds to address her as "Diane".

Of course, their private relationship is fully exposed in Season 4's "vs. Seduction Impossible" (though an anonymous male companion in bathrobe appears foraging through Beckman's refrigerator during an emergency midnight briefing from her home in Season 3 [vs. Tooth]). The episode opens with Montgomery leaving a romantic phone message for Diane while seated in a Moroccan bar: "I need to hear your voice tonight…I'm thinking of you. Sweet dreams, and besos [kisses in Spanish], my flower." Devastated by his failure to keep a promise to "throw in the towel," return to D.C., and become a "normal couple" made twenty years prior, Beckman is caught on the briefing screen in an unguarded moment drowning her sorrows with liquor, which she furtively slides out of the frame before again pointedly replacing a strand straying from her tight bun behind an ear. After Beckman proceeds to assign Team Bartowski an "off-the-books" mission to retrieve Montgomery from Morocco, Chuck wonders aloud, "What is going on with the General? She's a hot mess." The episode ends with Beckman, her relaxed emotions pointedly figured by wearing her hair down, at the same Moroccan bar in which it began. Though both have changed their minds about settling down, Montgomery voices hopes of future rendezvous…and Beckman "high hopes for Morocco tonight."

However, Beckman begins to progressively relax her interior walls to show sympathy and even concern in her relationship with the Castle Crew as well. Some signs of this transition are subtle. The general, though visibly perturbed, silently indulges Sarah's impetuous behavior when she is beside herself with grief over Chuck's abduction by The Belgian (vs. Phase Three). Likewise, she demonstrates some sensitivity to Chuck after the fiasco of naively enabling Frost and Volkoff to blow up Orion's secret base, claiming the only reason she doesn't have him "ejected from the Agency" is that the mission uniquely involved his mother (vs. First Fight & vs. Fear of Death). Additional early subtle gestures include notifying Sarah when law enforcement officials will arrive to pick up her father (giving her the ability to send him for ice cream) and, instead of returning Casey's salute, extending a hand and using Casey's first name… while dismissing him from the NSA (vs. Tic Tac).

Starting in the second half of Season 3, lapses in Beckman's professional detachment become more frequent. When Chuck shows signs of reneging on his first assignment as a real agent based in a European villa, Beckman, instead of cynically berating him, instead shows a softer touch. After acknowledging "the hand-wringing and the second-guessing are all part of [his] process," she gives him a week to go anywhere and do anything on the government's dime before expecting him to report to duty (vs. American Hero). And although she tries to prevent Chuck and Sarah from notifying her that they are "dating exclusively" upon their tardy return from Europe and Shaw's 'death' (vs. Honeymooners), Beckman, giving them a relatively mild lecture on the dangers involved, signs off with a rare glimpse of her personal feelings: "…Off the record, it's about damn time." Perhaps the general's most emotionally transparent moment, however, occurs when a distraught Sarah is faced with the possibility of Chuck's descent into madness (vs. Tooth). After assuring her, "Know that we will do everything we can for him," she confesses, with unprecedented sympathy in tone and expression, "I care about him, too."

Ultimately, Beckman fully lets her hair down, metaphorically speaking, with the Castle Crew as well as with Roan Montgomery. Though Chuck shows surprise that his superior enjoys sharing drinks with Condie Rice after hours during Season 2 (vs. Best Friend), the general turns out to be one of Team Bartowski's most loyal and trusted friends before the curtain drops on "Chuck". The shift begins in some ways when Beckman offers Chuck a job as an analyst not once but twice when he no longer possesses the Intersect (vs. Ring & vs. Phase III), claiming, "You're an asset with or without it." However, the relationship is tested in the most severe manner time and again when the general provides key aid to help Carmichael Industries take down Clyde Decker and even Shaw in Season 5.

In "vs. Cliffhanger", Beckman gives Chuck her personal key card, enabling him to enter Castle and obtain the Night Hawk prototype he uses to reach Decker in time to retrieve Volkoff/Hartley, before he disappears forever, and save Sarah. Similarly, in "vs. Frosted Tips" the general proactively seeks out Chuck to show him a top-secret file that reveals the hit order placed on the Morgansect. Before she leaves, she urges, "Protect your friend, Chuck," words one cannot imagine leaving her mouth in earlier seasons, especially in regards to the Bearded One.

By the time "vs. Curse" rolls around, Beckman is all in. Not only does she furtively warn the Castle Crew of an impending ambush through use of Morse Code during her faux briefing reprimand, but she arranges a rendezvous at the Roadside Café to reveal the conspiracy to destroy Chuck and plan a strategy. Of course, the supreme moment comes during "vs. Santa Suit" when she vows, "This is my team. And nobody, especially Shaw, is going to take *us* down." And her commitment is sealed with a kiss, literally. After informing Chuck the only way to infiltrate the CIA headquarters and retrieve the Macau Device is "with me" at the annual holiday party, the general saves the mission by improvising a make-out session with Chuck, while he is dressed as Santa no less, in Decker's office. Still the thorough professional, she calmly touches up her lipstick in the aftermath while matter-of-factly declaring, "We never speak of this again."

In the final episode of "Chuck", Beckman advises Casey that to succeed in making Quinn "very dead" she needs "Old Casey,...The Colonel" (vs. Goodbye). These words, however, come only after acknowledging that "five years in Burbank could turn a man to butter." In retrospect, one can make the argument that she was talking, at least partly, from personal experience. But despite unshrugging on the emotional front, she still manages to keep the world from rolling off her shoulders.

CHAPTER 8: LESTER

Trapeze Act

"Lucky for you, my Tuesday trapeze class was canceled." Most Chucksters would find themselves hard-pressed to identify this speaker on the first or second try. Perhaps Morgan after finishing his pole dancing class with Chuck? Or Devon, bored when his stationary cycling no longer offers an adrenaline rush? Try Lester. At first glance, the line seems like a throwaway, a humorous tidbit inserted merely to set a light-hearted mood for the comical Nerd Herders' service call at Devon's apartment (vs. Phase III). But the deeper one studies the enigmatic Mr. Patel, perhaps the most difficult character in the series to profile, the more the trapeze metaphor emerges as the text's most suitable figure for imaging a character, no matter how hilarious, whose personality swings back and forth in a dramatic fashion that doesn't always cohere. Indeed, in acting out his internal conflicts Lester displays such psychological gymnastics that he oftentimes resembles a careening acrobat needing someone to catch him before he takes a plunge.

Perhaps it is best to begin by chronicling Lester's slew of insecurities, for they form a frame through which to view other aspects of his character. On one hand, the Brown Beauty struggles with satisfying parental expectations. Raised with high-minded goals to achieve, he bemoans the "impossible standards" set for him in his childhood home (vs. The Ex). When he did not meet those expectations, a "version" of the Wheel of Misfortune, similar to the one he foists upon the Buy Morons while assistant manager, evidently awaited (vs. Seduction). Given the universally cruel consequences offered by Lester's wheel at the Buy More, ranging from "You're Fired" to "Diaper Station Duty", it is not surprising that Lester found his parents' prototype "very effective" in encouraging compliance. Intriguingly, Lester's familial conflict resurfaces late in the series. When crediting everyone from his "rep" to Jeff prior to screening his video montage 'masterpiece', the hesitant manner in which he includes his "parents…ish" suggests only limited or grudging appreciation (vs. Last Details).

Parental pressure extends to Lester's religious observance, too. Uniquely, Lester's family originally hails from the Hin-Jew colony inhabiting the Canadian plains of Saskatchewan, perhaps having broken off from the sister clan of his Montreal-based potential replacement (vs. Hack Off). Throughout the series, Lester repeatedly identifies with this sect, referring to his bar mitzvah (vs. Crown Vic), his inability to work in fast food due to keeping kosher (vs. First Kill), and his refusal to work on Shabbos (vs. Sensei). Moreover, he shows familiarity, respectively, with "the Parcheesi of [his] people" involving a dreidel and the traditional pancakes called latkas (vs. Crown Vic). In fact, the "Hebrew friend's" identity proves sufficiently important for him to object to Big Mike calling the annual Buy More celebration a Christmas Party in Season 1 and wears a yarmulke to the Season 5 version of the party in the fountain courtyard (vs. Santa Suit).

At the same time, a conflicted Lester shows signs of distancing himself from the exclusive religious roots of his "control freak" parents (vs. Balcony), cynically terming the colony "a cult of sorts." The erstwhile Hin-Jew not only cheats when gambling with a dreidel, ironically demanding, "Don't question my spirituality" (vs. Crown Vic), but contradicts his own Kosher practice when admitting he considers his faith's "dietary restrictions…obsolete" (vs. Balcony). Furthermore, he interprets his parents' intent to arrange his marriage to a Hin-Jewess as evidence of "dated traditions," consequently regarding them as "stuck in the ways of the old country." Instead, he claims to have "embraced America and its great traditions, like online dating…." Thus, Lester carries with him not only angst over meeting familial religious obligations but seems unanchored in terms of his own evolving religious mores.

Additional evidence suggests that Lester struggles with his sense of masculinity. The "scrawny ass Indian kid with a Bay City Rollers hairdo" (vs. Cougars) is further told he has the "hips of a 6-year-old girl" (vs. Living Dead). This physical profile apparently leaves Butterman confused when challenged to bring Morgan women's underpants to win concert tickets (vs. Third Dimension). Reaching into Lester's pants, the dense green shirt strips a pair off his traumatized co-worker, who is left declaring, "I'm a man! For god's sake, I'm a man!" The same basic concept lurks beneath Lester's "Fight Club" response to Chuck's kick to his face (vs. Operation Awesome). Besides telling Chuck it made him feel alive, he claims, "It made me feel like a man, maybe for the first time since my bar mitzvah," and he later exhorts those around the cage, "Who's next? Who wants to regain their manhood?" Is it surprising, then, that he enters prison claiming, after months of hitting the weights, he will come out looking "like a Hin-Jew Michelangelo"? (vs. Hack Off).

Lester's search for and reclamation of masculinity seemingly coincides with at least occasional ambivalence over gender identity and sexual orientation issues. When not "killing it" by attracting 4's in his online dating (vs. Balcony) or noting "God and the surgeon working in harmony" while recording with his mammary cam (vs. Marlin), the self-proclaimed "Brown Beauty" (vs. Beard) reads women's magazines at the Nerd Herd desk (vs. American Hero), studies how to survive on the Inside by watching a women's prison movie (vs. Hack Off), and finds it "oddly comfortable running in heels" and nylons when cross-dressing for his faux espionage mission tailing Devon. Speaking of Devon, Lester proves disappointed when Devon leaves the poker game fully clothed, repeating, "We've got to get that guy's pants off" (vs. Undercover Lover). And when Lester isn't admitting to Emmett that he Wonders What Chuck's Doing Right Now (vs. Tom Sawyer), he's telling Ellie that he "recognize[s] Chuck's sensual mouth" on her face (vs. Undercover Lover).

Lester further shows concern about a future without a mate or family of his own. When watching Chuck kiss Hannah at the Buy More, he looks on longingly while emphatically voicing his thoughts: "I am *so* lonely" (vs. Fake Name). The Nerd Herder even warns Chuck he will only lay off Hannah if the next hire is his wife, "a woman of color, preferably" (vs. Nacho Sampler). However, after observing the effect of Ellie's alleged affair on Devon (vs. Living Dead), Lester ironically swings in the opposite direction, insisting he will "choose NOT to be married" and will "ward [women] off," though his words may well drip with self-delusion. The Nerd Herder also gives indications that he fears he will not experience fatherhood. When stay-at-home-dad Devon visits the Buy More in Season 5 (vs. Frosted Tips), "Uncle Lester" melts while watching Baby Clara, telling her, "I am going to take a knife and fork and just eat those chubby little cheeks." And when Devon returns to reclaim Clara,

Lester, longing for "five more minutes," is left muttering, "Biological clock is tick-tocking."

Additional insecurities are explicitly noted. In one regard, he fears people. In the aftermath of one of his assistant manager debacles, Lester asks Morgan why he is helping him even though he treated him so poorly (vs. Cougars). The reply is crucial: "I thought…if I was there for you selflessly, that you would see that people are essentially kind at heart,… and maybe you wouldn't walk around so afraid in this world." The words, and the grace behind them, reduce Lester to tears. Likewise, the Hin-Jew fears taking risks…and the failure that may result. Lester can't follow through with performing the initial audition Jeff wrangles out of Devon for their wedding reception. At the time he concocts rationalizations about the alleged problems success will bring them but later softly whispers, "The truth is I was just sc-" (vs. Best Friend). Jeff doesn't let him finish.

Ironically, Lester's internal turmoil likely extends to a sense of underachievement, too, given his at times impressive display of intelligence. Confirming Big Mike's back-handed observation, "There may be a brain under that mop after all!" (vs. Ring Part II), Lester shows uncommon familiarity with literature and even history. On two occasions, Lester quotes the poetry of Walt Whitman ("Oh Captain, my Captain") when addressing Buy More superiors (vs. First Kill & vs. Pink Slip) and shows a fondness for recreating Alexander Dumas' *The Three Musketeers* ("All for one and one for all") when angling to give the impression of loyalty (vs. Beard). The allusions continue with a paraphrase of poet John Lyly ("All's fair in love and war") when hitting on Sarah in "vs. Hard Salami" and a quote from Shakespeare when taunting Chuck in "vs. Sandworm" ("Heavy is the head that wears the crown"). In perhaps his most noteworthy recitation, Lester, with sophisticated nuance, implies both his religious heritage and the espionage theme when revealing the Castle Crew as spies by shouting Emile Zola's famous phrase "J'Accuse!" which begins the author's expose of the anti-Semitic Dreyfus Affair involving the charge of spying (vs. Bo). On a different note, Lester single-handedly fixes Orion's uber Roark 7 computer for Devon and alleges his ability to hack the password in another 12 hours (vs. Phase III).

Lester's unsettled psyche, the sum of these various insecurities, is imaged nowhere more vividly than the uniquely unguarded moment afforded the viewer in his bedroom (vs. First Class). Moments before the publicly rebellious Nerd Herder is abducted by Casey for brainwashing to make him compliant at work, the frame presents the private Lester as a child pointedly lying under the covers in footie pajamas and snuggling a stuffed elephant to his chest. Startled from his sleep, appeal filling his eyes, the only word that manages to escape his mouth is a panicked "Mama?"

Ultimately, Lester's inability to master his anxieties appears to lead to a self-loathing that voices itself in dramatic irony. When Morgan suggests he should just be himself to impress Anna, Lester disagrees: "You have to be bet-ter than yourself, by like a factor of ten" (vs. Crown Vic), an assessment that echoes his own parentally-focused angst and foreshadows the misguided attempt to win the Hin-Jewess' affection by impressing her with a Bedouin mirage (vs. Balcony). Likewise, Lester ignorantly taunts Casey's masculinity and significance, accusing him of playing "make believe" about being a "tough military guy" and insisting "the truth is you're really just a shmuck who works at an electronics store" (vs. Final Exam). He probably couldn't have described his deepest feelings about himself any bet-ter.

In view of Lester's insecurities, complicated by his apparent self-loathing, the severe swings in his psychological trapeze act make a bit more sense. Seemingly, the loosely connected set of alternately pathetic and despicable behaviors Lester exhibits constitute often misguided and even reflexive responses triggered by his internal turmoil. In one regard, Lester flips his challenged self-esteem into masks of self-assuredness. On the purely comical level, he attempts to project a cool persona by slicking back his hair, swigging lime juice he mistakes for liquor (vs. Honeymooners), and posturing in interviews, like his Godfather turn in an interview with Chuck that trails off because he apparently forgets the words. He also jumps at the opportunity to ride on someone else's tails, as when parroting phrases in Big Mike's speech when he quells a Buy More riot (vs. Cubic Z).

On a more concerning level, however, Lester repeatedly displays an outward bravado that, when push comes to shove, proves a thin veneer when painfully stripped away. His Casanova imitations serve as Exhibit A. The minute Lester deems Sarah on the dating market, he strolls over to the Wienerlicious to ask if she would like to "grab a bi-te" (vs. Hard Salami). Overlooking the fact that she doesn't quite remember his name (Larry) and balks at the timing of his proposition (the day after his friend broke up with her), he proceeds to suavely whisper, "All is fair in love and war, Sarah." Taking him at his word, a mischievous Sarah leaps up on to the counter and, after sliding towards him with legs wrapped around his, suggests she "devour [him] right here." With panicked eyes, Lester peels himself away, promising to consider the idea even while creating a phantom pretext for his immediate and hurried departure. Similarly, Lester, slouched back in a chair and his feet propped up on a desk, has the audacity to summon Greta 4 to the cage for a Subway sandwich via the PA system before placing his hands behind his back with satisfaction: "Now we wait" (vs. Fear of Death). By the time Casey narrowly saves him from the knife-wielding assassin, an emotionally tumbling Lester admits he "needs a change of trousers."

Lester doesn't have any more success when trying to impress males. Pushed to the edge with the "Fight Club" rebellion led by Lester, Assistant Manager Morgan lays down the three basic rules of the Buy More. The sunglass-wearing rabble rouser, smirking with arms folded, taunts Morgan, claiming he doesn't have "the cojones" to enforce the third rule (firing). But when Morgan sets him straight and strolls away, the sun glasses come off immediately, and Lester follows, his smirk replaced with a tense smile, claiming it was all just "a little fun." Morgan doesn't let him off the hook, though, and the fierce Fight Clubber's façade ultimately somersaults into desperate pleading for his job in front of his posse, his palms outstretched: "For God's sake, Man, I got nowhere else to go!" The tears begin to well. "I *got* nowhere else to *go*...." After another pause, Morgan rehires him, and a subdued Lester doesn't even try to hide his relief or challenge his probation.

In perhaps its most juvenile turn, Lester's contorted psyche invests him with a "talent" for being "uniquely wasteful and destructive" (vs. Bullet Train). Of course, the examples could fill a book by themselves, so a few must suffice. In a scene recalling pre-adolescent rebellion, the 20-something responds to being informed of "the word that cannot be spoken" (pineapple) by repeating it three times while staring defiantly into Morgan's face (vs. Nemesis). Morgan's response speaks for many viewers: "Really?" Four years later, Lester still admits to sugaring gas tanks with regularity and plans to blow up an avocado in a Buy More microwave before stopped (vs. Bullet Train). In between, Lester takes satisfaction in offending customers with hostility simply for asking questions, and signs for Chuck's computer (from Orion) before almost incinerating a couple of Buy Mores with its new Predator "game" in Jeff's office (vs. Predator). Perhaps most telling, when Morgan turns his life around to become the "focused, responsible, driven" manager of the Buy More (vs. Tooth), Lester deems him to reside "in a very bad place."

But Lester's devious deeds escalate to various forms of cheating and lying. In a transparent moment, Lester advises Big Mike to handle a Buy More emergency by doing what he himself "rarely" does: "Tell. The. Truth" (Ring Part II). Where to start? While playing the Parcheesi of his people (vs. Crown Vic), the Hin-Jew first exploits his ignorant co-workers, clueless over the meaning of the "squiggly things" (Hebrew letters) on the dreidel. After glancing around and realizing no one knows he spun a hay, Lester hastily claims he spun a gimel and grabs a fistful of dollars. The Brown Beauty rakes in more cash by parading The Snake, knowing he can unhinge his jaw to stuff apples in his mouth (vs. Beard), and "saving" a wheelchair-bound Jeffrey Barnes who pleads for donations (vs. Zoom). Matters get downright criminal when the Nerd Herder falsifies sales numbers with the intent of winning the Salesman of the Year plumb: a trip to the Riverside convention (vs. Business Trip).

It doesn't take long for his deception to graduate to the level of company "traitor" either (vs. Alma Mater). After playing the role of co-conspirator in lifting the keys to Harry Tang's locker (and thus the Remote That Controls Them All), Lester plays Benedict Arnold and gleefully receives his new Buy More polo from Tang even while Morgan is sentenced to The Hole. A season later, Lester takes Morgan for a fool again (vs. Break-up). As Mitt and the Mighty Jocks stroll into the Buy More for payback, Morgan finally finds his spine and, turning to Lester, offers a call to camaraderie: "Do you want to do this?" With jaw set, lips pursed and eyes staring straight into Morgan's, Lester replies with a vow: "Let's do this." After they seal their bond with a hearty clasp of hands over the Nerd Herd counter, Morgan turns to confront the adversary… suddenly alone. Meanwhile, his alleged ally ducks behind the counter.

And the beat goes on. In his first routine interview with Emmett, the "Ass-kisser" offers to "grease the cogs" while offering the assistant manager $5 (vs. Tom Sawyer), and in a subsequent secret meeting, when Emmett is actually looking for dirt on Chuck, Lester makes clear he doesn't have an ethical dilemma with ratting Chuck out; he just doesn't know anything (vs. Fat Lady). Most despicably, Lester breaks ranks when The Ring operatives pose as buyers for the store. Extending his hand for others in the huddle to grasp, the would-be musketeer claims, "One for all and all for one" before assuring his fellow Buy Morons, "I love you guys." Still, the moment he enters the office he throws down not a gauntlet but his premeditated demand: "Before I spill this place's dirty secrets, I want to know that I'm protected. I want diplomatic immunity.... If you want dirt, I want immunity!" (vs. Beard).

When not selling others out, Lester displays elements of the Napoleonic Complex, also known as Little Man's Syndrome. The Nerd Herder proves a master of self-promotion and keeps track of where he stands in the social pecking order. When asked by Chuck about the Wikipedia entry on himself listed on his resume, a pursed-lipped Lester explains, "I have a certain following" (vs. First Date). And the moment that Morgan announces his departure from the Buy More, the Brown Beauty calls dibs on his locker, citing its location as "more prestigious than my own" (vs. Other Guy). It surprises no one, then, that upon his promotion to assistant manager, he publicizes the event with a store-sized banner hanging over the entry exterior: "Under New Assistant Management!" (vs. Seduction).

But Lester's just warming up. Once he ascends to ass man, he lords his authority over others in such a fascist manner that he is rechristened "Mussolini...drunk with power" (vs. Break-up). During his introduction to his former colleagues, El Duce announces he is to be addressed as Mr. Patel, Boss or, for Latin friends, "El Heffe" (vs. Seduction). And when his dictatorial management style runs into resistance, he vows, "If you're not going to respect me, you will fear me" while presenting the aforementioned Wheel of Misfortune. After Morgan is fired on the first spin, it leads to the entire staff quitting. However, even as the Buy Morons file out, Lester tries to cover his rejection with more false assertions of power: "Who needs you? You're fired! Do I have your attention now?!" But the room is already empty. To his credit, though, the trapeze artist proceeds to flip his leadership persona after another Buy More humiliation: "I just want to acknowledge that I'm not the easiest man to work for, but I want to thank you for all your hard work and mean it this time" (vs. Cougars). Perhaps coming to his senses, he submits his ass man resignation, effective immediately.

In a final facet of the Little Man's Syndrome, Lester occasionally proves vengeful when his attempts at gaining respect fail. After Assistant Manager Morgan exposes the limits of Lester's "Fight Club" rebellion,

Lester sets a variety of booby traps around the Buy More, going so far as to pretend he is sitting in the chair he vacates prior to Morgan's becoming glued to it (vs. First Class). In more muted fashion, Lester agrees to drop legal action against Casey's violation of the "no touching" policy (i.e. ramming Jeffster's heads together) only after the demands for Casey paying for their Subway lunches and taking a bite from Jeff's sub is added to his apology (vs. Final Exam).

Given the emotional acrobatics of the Trapeze Act, it is particularly fitting that the text also presents him as a "tortured artist" (vs. Best Friend). If anything, Lester expresses an alternative artistic vision that graphically evidences his conflict. In Season 3, he offers an ineffective and unappreciated "free-form, no-hold-barred poetry slam" in an attempt to diffuse a Buy More riot, invoking McFly, no less (vs. Cubic Z). A bit later, the Hin-Jew "comes clean" and reveals "the real Lester: uncut, unabridged…in living color" (vs. Balcony). However, the leather outfit combined with a grooving buttocks and aggressive facial expressions only succeeds in producing "the most uncomfortable five minutes" of the Hin-Jewess' life. These efforts, though, prove downright tame compared to the montage movie-making style Lester unveils at the end of Season 4 (vs. Last Details).

Sporting a sloppy ascot, the "auteur," who insists on the "first and final cut" of Charah's rehearsal dinner surprise, becomes overwhelmed with emotion even before his flick begins to roll. At first, the scene presents Devon and Ellie smiling while a romantic soundtrack compliments the sentimental images that flow across the screen. But the mood shifts suddenly when a jump-suited Lester superimposes himself into the frame, a heart held over his genitalia. To the tiny audience's horror, he begins to pogo up and down even as he digresses into gibberish: "Heart. Pancreas. Cockle. My cockle." Soon, demonic facial expressions replace normal ones as Lester continues, "Shippy, shippy, shippy." Finally, he screeches, "America!" and faux vomits before the performance's sudden and premature termination. Lester's response to the Woodcombs proves equally telling. Informed, "That is just unholy!" he replies, with a pleased smile, "Thank you."

As the series nears its conclusion, viewers rightfully wonder if there is hope for Mr. Patel's transition to a less conflicted reality based on something more productive than a raft of insecurities. Indeed, the Trapeze Act seems on a course to continue his wobbly, reactive performance, one that just may end with a disastrous plunge. Thankfully, though, there is one standing by who himself has only recently become equipped to reach out, catch him, and coax him off the bar (See Chapter 15: The Flames of Destiny).

Chapter 9: Reading the Visual Text

Part I: Prop-ositions

When does an object or action on the screen represent something more than its surface function? In the case of "Chuck", the answer is more often than you might think. Those closely following the series eventually come to realize that few actions or images upon which the camera lens focuses are merely the product of chance. After re-watching scenes, episodes, seasons, and even the entire show, the observant viewer discovers recurring visual patterns in the use of props and cinematography that fit specific contexts, subtly adding texture to the surface action by metaphorically developing the characters involved.

On one level, the use of hand or mobile props permeates the show. In one distinct motif, the books with which characters are associated provide imaginative insights into their core traits. Chuck is actually linked to two books, including *Y: The Last Man* in multiple episodes. Calling the graphic novel (aka comic series) "the greatest literary achievement of our generation," he hides behind the cover while sliding Manoosh his Nacho Sampler in the episode of the same name. The cover also earns a place of permanent honor in Chuck's room, framed in a niche behind his computer near the Tron poster. Written by Brian K. Vaughan, *Y: The Last Man* contains notable parallels to Chuck's life. Not only is the protagonist, Yorick Brown, the last man on Earth, recalling Chuck's unique Intersect identity, but Brown falls in love with Agent 355, the female government agent assigned to protect him, directly imitating Chuck's romantic liaison with Agent Walker. Moreover, Brown has a constant companion in his pet monkey, mirroring Chuck's relationship with Morgan, who is actually figured as an ape on the Buy More flat screens in Season 3 while retrieving the "Planet of the Apes" DVD for Casey (vs. Tic Tac).

The show foregrounds another Vaughan comic book series title, *Ex-Machina*, for similar purposes (vs. Predator). Near the end of Season 2, when a desperate Chuck seeks to extract the Intersect from his head in order to resume a normal, non-computerized life, he takes the schematics to the Roark Instruments plant and glues them into a copy of the comic book so he can study them even while under surveillance. However, beyond a mere plot device the act also links Chuck to the series' super-hero protagonist, called "The Great Machine", who voluntarily seeks to abandon his super powers to, as the title suggests, become an ex-machine.

This novel technique is used to develop a few other characters as well. Jeff, soon after his dramatic transformation from mostly moronic to bright, underscores this change by reading a significant book at the Nerd Herd desk (vs. Business Trip). In his hands, he holds Daniel Keyes' *Flowers For Algernon*, a novel in which the protagonist, as part of a scientific experiment, grows from a relatively stupid soul capable of working only a menial job into an extremely intelligent individual smarter than those who used to look down on him. Alas, the novel ends on a less optimistic note than the show: the protagonist's metamorphosis turns out to be only temporary, as he regresses back to his former state.

The portrayal of Ellie uses the same developmental device. While she works at the dining room table on the computer Orion left for her, pointedly framed over Devon's shoulder, her husband reads aloud a portion of Richard Leakey's *Origins: The Emergence and Evolution of Our Species and its Possible Future* on the couch, allegedly to Baby Clara (vs. Family Volkoff). The text, discussing "missing links" and fossil specimens "in a state of intermediary development," clearly isn't a children's story, though. Instead, the anthropological study perfectly figures Ellie's intermediary development as she proceeds to restore missing links with her parents and evolve into an impressive neurobiologist by researching the files on Orion's computer, ultimately becoming part of Team Bartowski.

General Beckman and Shaw join the book club, too, though they are not actually seen holding any volumes. Comically claiming the bill Chuck rings up for his attempted rescue of Sarah from Shaw at the desert warehouse weighs more than her copy of *Atlas Shrugged*, the comment subtly suggests the more serious idea that the responsibility of protecting citizens in a violent world rests on her shoulders as a high-ranking officer in the NSA (vs. American Hero). In contrast, the books in Shaw's loft library, pointedly panned by the camera, connect to a pair of his traits (vs. Living Dead). While *Zen Buddhism: A History* meshes with his uncanny ability to remain calm in the midst of crises, copies of *The Guide to Getting it On* and the *Karma Sutra* reinforce his sexually-oriented pursuit of Sarah.

Books aren't the only props characters in "Chuck" can hold in their hands. In the pilot, Chuck famously tells Sarah on their first 'date' that he will be happy to serve as her "very own baggage handler" after she admits she just ended a long relationship and "may come with baggage." Thus begins another standard visual trope in the series, the baggage motif, to figure emotional turmoil. Not surprisingly, Sarah is the one primarily linked to these images. The most obvious occurrence comes in Season 3, which includes an extended focus upon her difficulty, because of her itinerant childhood, in unpacking her suitcase and establishing a permanent home (vs. Suitcase), whether living in her hotel room or moving in with Chuck.

However, the motif pops up on multiple occasions to figure other internal conflicts she faces as well. When unable to tell Chuck the real issue behind her need to travel to Hungary and confront Ryker, because she was taught to not trust others, Sarah pointedly stows materials in a bag she then closes and slings over her shoulder, prepared to leave Castle alone (vs. Baby). However, when she finally agrees to let Chuck and Casey join her private mission on a no-questions-asked basis, partially unburdening herself, she notably lets the bag fall with a thump to the ground, though it remains full.

"Vs. Goodbye" utilizes a similar image. Plagued with amnesia, Sarah is on the verge of leaving Castle for Berlin in search of Quinn by herself while wracked with confusion over her real identity: Agent Walker or Sarah Bartowski. By no coincidence, she grabs a suitcase from the supply rack moments before she, with visible conflict, confesses to Chuck, "I can't be here. I don't know how to be the woman that you remember me as. All I know is how to be a spy. A good one. It's all I know how to do." But again, after accepting Chuck's plea to "help" with the mission, allowing the rediscovery process to continue until it ends on a Malibu beach, Sarah exits Castle without a second thought about the suitcase she just hauled off the rack.

A couple of more clever variations to the motif are worth noting. Chuck's invitation of the C.A.T. squad to their engagement party stems from his concern about Sarah having friends present when Sarah herself has few qualms about it (vs. C.A.T. Squad). However, when Chuck proceeds to get too involved with handling what he perceives as Sarah's emotional issues during the episode, he is ultimately sent to retrieve the C.A.T. squad's luggage at the apartment simply so he will leave hers alone. Moreover, he struggles with the hefty load, dropping bags, implying both the size of the task and his inexpert job in handling it. Indeed, Ellie interrupts his burdened trek back to Castle to advise him he doesn't "need to fix everything" and to try seeing things from Sarah's perspective. By the end of the episode, after Sarah lets him know she's "not ready to dive into her past right now," he agrees to "stick to...[the] thousand other ways" in which Sarah needs and desires his help daily.

In Season 3, in the midst of Chuck and Sarah's estrangement, one finds a more subtle instance. Shaw brings a bag Sarah left in the car into Castle when they return from their trip to D. C. together and plops in on the conference table (vs. Final Exam). Equally interesting, Sarah, briefly taken aback, immediately stows it beneath the table, out of sight. Given the context, these seemingly insignificant details actually externalize an important element of Sarah's internal turmoil pertaining to Chuck. Since Shaw and Sarah's coupling advanced during the excursion, it not only suggests that Sarah's relationship with Shaw really constitutes an attempt to leave behind her baggage with Chuck but also indicates that her emotional burden will follow her wherever and with whomever she goes, even if she tries to conceal it on the outside. And since Shaw brings the bag into Castle, it may also extend to imply that their off-hours relationship complicates the working relationship the three share.

Sarah is not the only subject figured by the baggage motif, though. Also in Season 3, in the midst of his emotional estrangement from Sarah, Chuck prepares for a mission alone with her in Castle a couple of episodes after having realized his lingering feelings for Sarah (vs. Tic Tac). Pointedly stowing all his supplies into a pack, zipping it shut, and hoisting it on his back, he finally snaps the harness shut (vs. Tic Tac). Meanwhile his mouth remains mostly zipped while listening to Sarah, currently coupled with Shaw, softly acknowledge what he "sacrificed" to become a spy (i.e. their relationship when not running away with her in Prague) and urge him not to forget what makes him "great". Battling with whether and how to respond, Chuck finally decides to speak, but just as he begins Sarah, seemingly aware of her own vulnerability, cuts him off as a self-defense mechanism and changes the subject back to the mission, leaving a still-burdened Chuck standing with a full pack.

Orion takes his turn in the rotation, too. Upon her father's surprise arrival at the apartment (vs. Dream Job), Ellie, ruminating over the pancakes he never made for her when he disappeared, storms out of the room, causing Chuck to hand his father, who is already carrying one bag, his other bag, too, before following his distraught sister. When Devon proceeds to hold out his hand to shake the hand of Orion, who now has both hands full, Orion instead hands him one of the bags. Accordingly, over a drink, Orion subsequently dumps his emotional baggage about being Ellie's delinquent father on Devon while his future son-in-law dumps his concerns about the bachelor party gone awry.

In contrast to the baggage motif, scenes using some form of eye glasses imply a pair of meanings. In one regard, they are used to accent the perspective a character gains in a particular episode. In Season 3, Chuck gains insight into his lingering feelings for Sarah after their drifting apart allows him the distance to see things clearly (vs. Fake Name). While pointedly peering into Shaw's hotel room at least half a mile away through the telescopic scope of Rafe Gruber's sniper rifle, and listening in with headphones, Chuck experiences an epiphany after observing Sarah reveal her real name and kiss Shaw: "Sam is…my girl, sorta." In fact, the very next scene finds him confessing to Ellie that he is "living a lie," and agreeing with her assessment that "the truth is that you still have feelings for Sarah." Later that same evening, Hannah is history.

The pattern alters slightly when other realizations are linked with sets of binoculars. While on the sentimental stake out prepared by Chuck for his alleged final spy test (vs. Final Exam), both Chuck and Sarah stare forward with the glasses to their eyes, supposedly looking for the mark to enter the hotel. However, Chuck, who already has changed his perspective (see above), expresses another epiphany when, after lowering his set, he corrects himself and admits that it was his decision in Prague that caused their separation. He then goes on to envision a future together if he can pass his spy test, and ends by asking if Sarah is willing to "give it another *shot*," alluding back to his insight gained via the sniper rifle. Sarah's answer is silent, but her assumption of a new perspective becomes clear nonetheless. Having already quietly acknowledged, "I know," when Chuck told her she will miss him when she permanently leaves for D.C. with Shaw, Sarah, visibly moved, finally lowers her own set of glasses. Turning to meet Chuck's gaze, she leans toward him to accept his kiss… until Shaw's urgent inquiries noting they missed the target's entry shatter the moment.

In Season 4, Casey and Sarah also reach separate epiphanies while together observing the entrance to Volkoff's Swiss Alps bunker with binoculars (vs. Family Volkoff). Discussing Chuck's "cool" response to signing the pre-nup she springs on him, Sarah lowers her pair of glasses to confess, "Now I see what Chuck's side of it would have been like: flipping out about a relationship based on the contents of an envelope…seeing the end before we've even started." Of course, she will eventually tear up the document. Simultaneous with Sarah's insight, Casey finds himself enlightened by Sarah's dilemma of being "caught between [divorced] parents," the reason for her pre-nup in the first place, and agrees that the "hardest place for a kid is right in the middle." Thus, Casey does an about-face on the issue of Alex's graduation day plans before the episode ends, insisting that they get together on another day, because "It's not fair for [her] to be torn between two parents."

Alternatively, the series uses eye glasses to distinguish between the cover identities and real identities of each member of the Castle Crew, but especially Sarah. On a couple of occasions, Sarah uses glasses simply to accent her cover, as when attending the Roark Instruments Expo as a nerd (vs. Dream Job) and acting as a secretary in the Lichtenstein scam (vs. DeLorean). However, their use becomes more nuanced in a few other scenes. Posing as a nurse at the Costa Gravan embassy, she wears them as long as she must keep up appearances with the unconscious premier's two guards armed with machine guns (vs. Angel del Muerte). The moment she finishes putting them in their own need of a hospital, though, the resurfacing Sarah borrows one of the machine guns, nonchalantly tosses the glasses aside, and urges, "Let's go," before walking out the door in search of Casey.

Sarah again dons glasses when portraying Dr. Eva Anderson to give a presentation at the scientific conference in Jill's place and keeps them on even while stalking the operative who contaminates the hall (vs. Ex). However, when she returns from killing the rogue agent the glasses are pointedly missing when Sarah, not Dr. Anderson, appears visibly uncomfortable while watching Jill and Chuck embrace after they emerge safely from the hall. Similarly, though Sarah wears glasses while posing as hostess of an outdoor café and Chuck deals for the Atroxium with Dr. Wheelright in Season 4, she pointedly discards them before running to Chuck as his concerned lover after he is shot by Frost and lies sprawled on the ground (vs. Aisle of Death).

Sometimes the use of hand props focuses as much on the manner in which the objects are used as the objects themselves. A few key scenes rely on rearrangement imagery to figure the internal rearrangement of a character's priorities or emotions. Sarah's internal reorganization of priorities between her latent hope of a future normal life with family and the adventurous spy life in which she feels secure finds expression in "vs. Santa Claus". Prior to Chuck walking in to the Orange Orange with an invitation to Christmas Eve at the Bartowskis, the camera pointedly focuses on Sarah's redistribution of empty cups and tongs along the glass fixture just before she stops to ponder the advertisement promoting holiday family fun on the far wall. As a whole, the visual imagery implies that Sarah is prepared to rearrange her life if necessary to hold on (tongs) to her dream of family, which she ultimately wants to fill up her relatively vacant life (empty cups), at least emotionally speaking. Accordingly, she not only proceeds to accept Chuck's gesture of giving her the bracelet as his "real" girlfriend, unlike her prior rejection of a similar gesture in the Season 1 finale (joining him to congratulate the Woodcombs on their engagement), but she kills the rogue agent who threatens the future the gift promises, the bracelet prominently dangling from her wrist.

In a similar manner, an amnesia-plagued Sarah rearranges the cups and straws in the Berlin Wienericious in "vs. Goodbye" to conform with their typical arrangement years before at the Burbank location. Though it suggests her memory is slowly returning, it more importantly implies the internal rearrangement of her feelings for Chuck as they begin to shift from cynicism back to their former state. Immediately prior, her lips hover near his while they dance at the gala, and she is forced to squelch a charmed smile while Chuck recalls their first 'date' at the El Compadre knock-off. By the end of the episode, she's kissing him on the beach.

The rearrangement motif features a key scene involving Ellie as well, but it conveys a different type of struggle. When hosting her estranged mother for lemonade at the apartment, Ellie betrays frustration with the coasters, which figure the fear of her absentee parent further 'staining' her heart. Just as Ellie struggles with where to place them on the coffee table, noting she doesn't usually use them, she agonizes over both how to protect herself, something she rarely finds herself doing, and how to configure her conflicting feelings during the bittersweet reunion (vs. First Fight).

One of the easiest personal props to miss is the pair of images (at least) involving the removal of an object that lingers on Chuck's person to represent the emotional residue from which he is having difficulty freeing himself in that scene. In Season 1, Chuck struggles with the prospect of returning to Stanford for a mission due to the hurtful memories he still carries from his experience there: Bryce Larkin's getting him kicked out of school and Jill's dumping him to be with Bryce. Before he gives Sarah the Chuck Bartowski Memorial Tour (vs. Alma Mater), Chuck significantly brushes off a leaf that falls on his shoulder while admitting, "This is really freaking me out. It's like nothing has changed." When asked by Sarah whether that's good or bad, Chuck proves so internally discombobulated that he can't even manage an answer beyond saying, "It's a...it's a...yeah."

A matching image appears in "vs. Aisle of Terror". Dazed by the brief yet violent reappearance of his delinquent mother after years of absence, Chuck tries to console himself by suggesting, "She may be a bad mom, but she makes a great spy, right?...I guess it doesn't matter; she's gone." When asked if he is OK, he replies, "I'm just wondering what to tell my sister....Do I casually drop that Mom came back to town to shoot me in the chest...?" Still distracted, Chuck walks through a faux spider's web moments later, part of the Buy More Halloween decor. He carries a cottony remnant on his shoulder for a few more paces before picking it off and tossing it to the side, the metaphorical equivalent of his attempt to move on emotionally unencumbered. As matters play out, that proves no easy task.

This, of course, is a far-from-exhaustive overview of the series' penchant for hand or mobile props. Even a selective analysis of some of these devices, though, proves sufficient to demonstrate the depth of the series' textured visual text. But it's only the beginning.

CHAPTER 10: READING THE VISUAL TEXT

Part II: Cinematography & Stage Props

In addition to the objects characters possess or manipulate, visual texts utilize a variety of camera effects to achieve complexity in plot, theme, and characterization. In most cases, these effects, like hand props, externalize or objectify an internal or subjective idea. "Chuck" implements quite an array of these with such consistency that the motifs, if identified, aid interpretation of the series. However, space allows for only a selective overview of both types and examples of those types. A full analysis would require multiple chapters or a book of its own.

A couple of visual effects connote some aspect of characters' phantom or double lives usually hidden from the view of others or perhaps even themselves. In the case of the reflection motif, one of the series' most common devices, interpretation of a specific mirror image depends on the nature and even stage of the respective character's secret identity. Devon's entry into the spy life at the end of Season 2 provides a simple example to grasp the basic concept behind this technique. When caught snooping in Casey's apartment by The Colonel, it triggers a string of events that ends with Chuck revealing his identity as a CIA asset as well as the identities of his handlers (vs. Colonel). As a result, Chuck gives Devon his first "mission": to "be cool" by keeping the secret and "handl[ing] Ellie". Thus assuming his own spy life hidden from Ellie, Devon returns home, where he pointedly stares at his reflection in the kitchen window above the sink, signifying his new double identity, while drawing and drinking a baptismal glass of water from the faucet. Though he mutters to himself, "Chuck's a spy; stay cool...stay cool," Devon has problems actually doing so when Ellie walks in.

Over the course of the series, Chuck is figured by up to a dozen different reflection images that imply a few variations of this basic double life concept, depending on the context in which they are found. In the first three episodes of Season 1, the images, similar to the one involving Devon above, contrast Chuck's normal civilian identity with his new secret identity as the Intersect. The first, found while he readies himself privately in front of the bathroom mirror for his first 'date' with Sarah, proves a bit ironic. Though confused over his initial flashes, which initiate his Intersect life, he remains ignorant of the secret spy life awaiting until it accosts him in the middle of that date. Thus the first reflection image of Chuck largely foreshadows his imminent entry into a double life (Pilot). In the second episode, Chuck, now all-too-aware of his spy identity, again dresses before a mirror in his room but this time with Ellie and Morgan looking on, both of whom remain ignorant of the real, espionage-related nature of the date. The mirror reflection in the third episode adds another bit of nuance: Chuck, dressing in a tux, assumes his just-created cover identity as Charles Carmichael for his first secret mission after having learned the tango from an unsuspecting Devon supposedly to enhance his 'date' with Sarah.

The dynamic continues in a different context later in Season 1 when Chuck stares at his reflection in the mirror at Casey's apartment (vs. Imported Hard Salami). While his handlers prepare him for an evening with Lou at a night club, which unknown to Lou will double as a mission investigating her ex-boyfriend, Chuck laments, "We're only on our second official date, and already I'm lying to her." In fact, Chuck's secret life will prove to complicate the normal civilian relationship they share to such an extent—along with his receipt of Sarah's impulsive kiss—that he feels compelled to end it by the end of the episode.

In contrast, the series finale creatively reverses this initial dynamic with another mirror image to figure instead the sufficiency of Chuck's real identity over his phantom one. At the urging of Ellie, Devon, Morgan and even Baby Clara, Chuck determines to get out of bed and win back an amnesia-plagued Sarah. While dressing in his room to begin this quest, he pointedly turns his back on the mirror as the lens focuses on his real person, not the partial reflection of his body visible behind him. Accordingly, Chuck, in a sign of growth, eschews any false identity to pursue his quest, including that of Charles Carmichael, in favor of his actual one, stating, "…She may be the best spy in the world, but I'm Chuck Bartowski. It's not like she's out of my league." This contrasting alternative approach is reprised earlier during Hartley's rediscovery of his real identity (vs. Cliffhanger). After the suppression of the Intersect eliminates his Volkoff identity, the lens presents Hartley staring into a hand mirror without ever showing Hartley's reflection, only his real face above the back of the mirror.

As the series progresses, additional reflection images focus on Chuck's rediscovery of either his latent civilian or spy identity. In "vs. First Date", Chuck dances on his bed with joy at the prospect of returning to a normal civilian life with the new Intersect almost online. Strolling into the bathroom, he wipes clean the fogged mirror to smile at his reflection, implying the seemingly imminent return to his original life. Of course, he is "blind" to the fact that this transition will not really occur given the assassination hit Beckman has ordered Casey to complete, as implied by Chuck's comic horror over seeing Ellie and Devon in the shower. But this dynamic is reversed in a similar image found at the beginning of Season 3. When the Intersect 2.0 is temporarily kicked out of the CIA after failing the spy school created for him (vs. Pink Slip), Chuck slides into a deep depression as he also fails to deal with the normal civilian life he once cherished. When he becomes inspired to again pursue the espionage life, the lens pointedly shows him in front of the same fogged mirror, wiping it clean while shaving off his beard. Accordingly, this reflection image ironically suggests his aspiration to leave his pathetic civilian existence and re-assume his spy identity as Charles Carmichael.

The reflection motif is not limited to figuring only the tension between Chuck's spy and civilian lives, however. One image in Season 3 appears in conjunction with Chuck's initiating a double life kept hidden from his fellow spy girlfriend Sarah. After his initial therapy session with Dr. Dreyfus reveals the Intersect has the ability to "overwhelm the mind" and leave the victim in a state "much akin to insanity" (vs. Tooth), a rattled Chuck is found washing his face in the bathroom sink. Looking up at his reflection in the mirror, he tries to assure himself, "You're not crazy. Don't freak out." But when Sarah enters to inquire about his appointment, Chuck proceeds to lie, saying it went "fine" rather than admit his benching or profound fears about his mental state, a secret he will keep in some form all the way to the end of the season.

A final set of reflection images portray Chuck as fooling himself into thinking he can enjoy a normal romance outside his spy existence. In these cases, however, the image is significantly different from those already noted above in that the reflection is disembodied from the subject:

Chuck's actual self is not included in the frame, implying the phantom reality has overtaken or detached from the actual one to leave him in a state of delusion. In the first of these, Chuck's reflected face fills up most of the frame in a close-up that omits everything but the bathroom mirror and its frame (vs. Imported Hard Salami). Smiling the day after a successful make-up date with Lou, he congratulates himself, "Morning, Handsome. Nice work last night." Chuck's self-satisfaction, though, is quickly exposed as a fantasy. For when dates turn into missions, Lou becomes a suspect, and Chuck cannot reveal his real identity to explain matters, the relationship proves unworkable with his spy life—or his rediscovered feelings for Sarah. Consequently, Lou is gone by the end of the episode.

Similarly, Season 2 presents Chuck's delusion in thinking his just-resumed relationship with Jill can coexist with his suppressed feelings for Sarah, his spy life, and Jill's own espionage identity, though he remains unaware of the latter for much of the arc (vs. Fat Lady). As a seemingly jealous Jill asks Chuck questions about the nature of his relationship with his cover girlfriend, the disembodied reflection of Chuck and Jill, her face hovering over his shoulder, fills the entire frame while he finishes dressing for a mission in front of a mirror. Their actual persons are never shown. Of course, Chuck's spy life again shatters the fantasy when Jill later misconstrues a pocket-dialed phone conversation and observes Chuck and Sarah half-naked in the hotel room after getting out of the shower. During that shower, the slo-mo footage also indicates the stirring of Chuck's submerged desires for Sarah. Ultimately, though, Jill's own rogue spy identity and betrayal completes Chuck's rude awakening to harsh reality.

Though smaller in scope, a set of reflection images also provides profound insight into Sarah's psychology. Since her core identity is that of a spy, unlike Chuck, the mirror images associated with Agent Walker externalize a different double life she keeps hidden from others and even herself: the dream of a future normal life including family and home. This latent reality is clearly figured in "vs. Wookiee" after she has stared into the goldfish bowl and before she has been prevented from stepping into the shower by a scuffle with a masked intruder that ends with the overturning of the fishbowl (For a full analysis of this scene and Sarah's pre-existing dream, see *Unpacking "Chuck"* Chapter 2: Fish Out of Water). In between, the lens pointedly presents the distinct reflection of

Sarah's face against the shower tiling, suggesting the conflict between the elements of her dual nature as she is already considering the possibility of a future with Chuck, though not ready to act on it.

The motif continues to develop Sarah's guarded dual nature at the start of Season 3. Estranged from Chuck, she dresses in front of the mirror with Carina for the engagement party mission (vs. Three Words). After disingenuously claiming that the charm bracelet Carina points out "isn't really my thing," a pensive Sarah, staring at her reflection, proceeds to ponder more honestly, "Do you ever wonder about a different life?" When Carina clarifies, "You mean like if all of this was real? If we were really getting ready for my engagement party?" Sarah confirms, "Yeah." The difference between the two spies becomes even more pronounced when Carina answers her own question firmly in the negative.

Even after Sarah and Chuck get together, reflection images indicate Sarah's hidden thoughts of the next step towards home and family: marriage. In "vs. Honeymooners", Chuck slips a faux ring on her finger as part of their cover to impersonate a married couple, leaving Sarah to merely stare ahead dreamily. But on the eve of their own engagement party, the lens suggests Sarah's deeply guarded dream has become much more tangible. Before Chuck enters the room, Sarah privately touches the engagement ring on her finger, the lens focused on its reflection in their bedroom mirror. The minute Chuck enters the room, she lets go of the ring, turns from the mirror and broaches a different topic, but she is still clearly thrilled with their pending union, ending the scene with a broad smile and saying, "Let's party."

In this context, the mirror imagery in "vs. Sarah" at the end of the series helps to interpret Sarah's amnesia-plagued mindset when she is about to run from Burbank at episode's close. Having just realized that Quinn lied and Chuck told the truth about their romance, and also just prior to viewing her video log with visible emotion, Sarah's identity crisis reaches a climax: is she CIA Agent Walker or Mrs. Sarah Bartowski? The issue is further accented at the start of the next episode when Sarah confesses to Chuck in Castle that she doesn't know how to be the woman he remembers, only a spy, prior to accepting his offer of help in Berlin. Accordingly, when Sarah rushes back and forth in the hotel between her reflection in the mirror, signifying her identity as Sarah Bartowski the lover, and her suitcase, signifying her identity as Agent Walker the spy, it externalizes her struggle and confusion over which is the real one.

In retrospect, these images suggest that the series' first reflection image of Sarah, when she dresses in front of the mirror of her hotel room for her first 'date' with Chuck (Pilot), may communicate a more complex reality than at first glance. Initially, one reasonably interprets it as simply the inverse equivalent to the same image used to figure Chuck: Agent Walker, donning poisoned hair pins, body armor, and ankle-strapped knife, will be assuming a double identity as cover girlfriend for the evening. However, Sarah later admits that she fell for Chuck sometime between fixing her phone, which has already occurred, and diffusing the bomb with a porn virus, which is about to occur (vs. Other Guy). Given this perspective, the reflection sequence in the pilot possibly takes on added texture.

The use of shadow effects, though more narrow in scope, complements the use of reflection imagery, for the shadows also imply a phantom or double existence. Devon again provides a simple example to illustrate the concept. After seeing how much sifting through the data found on Orion's computer means to Ellie, who finds the research invigorating as a new stay-at-home mom, Devon can't follow through with his agreement with Chuck to switch out the hard drive in an effort to protect her (vs. Muurder). Initiating a double life of his own, Devon meets Chuck in the courtyard to assure him, "It's done," and the computer is "Kaput." Immediately after lying to his brother-in-law, Devon returns to his apartment, the lens pointedly situated to capture his shadow on the wall preceding him into the living room. Proceeding to sit down next to Ellie, who is intently working on Orion's computer, Devon further highlights their new secret life: "So, we're still not telling Chuck, right?"

Another pair of shadows figure elements of Sarah's phantom existence. While infiltrating Volkoff's organization, Sarah is required to demonstrate her loyalty to him before he trusts her. Accordingly, Volkoff arranges a supreme test: killing 'former' colleague John Casey. Sarah is forced to assume a false identity for this purpose, one that remains hidden even from Chuck, who agonizes over Sarah's throwing Casey out a window to pass the test, though she secretly receives Casey's prior consent. Consequently, when Sarah reaches the top floor of the high rise to meet Casey, her silhouette precedes her along the wall, indicating that the Sarah showing up is a shadow not to be confused with the real one.

Volkoff, however, is fooled by her double performance and tells Chuck he's one step closer to the woman he loves.

The dynamic shifts a bit in the other shadow image. Sarah, struggling with amnesia, reacts violently to her identity confusion in "vs. Sarah" at the Dream House. When Chuck, who takes her there to spur her memory, brings Sarah to the verge of letting down her guard with his emotionally transparent appeal, her defense mechanisms kick back in. Upon striking him repeatedly in the face and kicking him down the stairs, Sarah follows her victim with the lens remaining focused on the wooden railing after she passes to emphasize the movement of her trailing shadow. The message? The woman abusing Chuck is but an impostor of Sarah Bartowski, who would not recognize her.

Creating shadows requires a somewhat sophisticated blend of lighting and camera positioning. However, less complex camera work in the series still packs subtle meaning. In "vs. Living Dead", Casey suggests reviewing the receipts from Shaw's trip to D.C. with Sarah, a period during which Chuck and Sarah were estranged, to see if Chuck can flash on anything that might lead them to Shaw. It proves an uncomfortable time for both Chuck and Sarah as they get to the bottom, so to speak, of the true nature of Sarah's relationship with Shaw, including the revelation of gourmet meals, a couple's massage, and even the purchase of Tiffany diamond ear rings. Accordingly, the lens begins the scene focused on nervously jiggling legs beneath the table (i.e. the bottom of things) before rising to a fixed position above the table.

The same bottom-to-top camera movement is found in Jeff's triumphant entry into the Buy More as a new man (vs. Frosted Tips). In this case, though, the technique suggests his difference is from head to toe as well as implying that he has arisen from the depths of his previously moronic behavior. Moreover, the camera proceeds to fully circle him, further suggesting the completeness of his transformation.

"Chuck" also occasionally utilizes camera angles to approximate a character's point of view, thereby revealing or accenting their mindset. A matching pair of examples suffices to illustrate the show's broader use of the technique, including one again focused on the Sarah of the series' finale arc. Newly arrived in Echo Park on her mission from Quinn, Sarah's emotional defenses remain on high alert as she stalks the husband she thinks served only as her mark in prior years (vs. Sarah). When Chuck, distraught over the distance he senses with Sarah, seeks out

Ellie to unburden himself, Sarah follows to listen, knife in hand, from the upstairs hallway. The scene pointedly inserts camera shots from Sarah's point of view as she looks down on them from above among standard shots of both Chuck and Ellie on the couch and Sarah upstairs. Moreover, the views from Sarah's perspective portray her guarded psyche by having the lens peer through the wrought iron of the guard rail at the beginning and end of the scene. In between, when her guard is lowered by Chuck's tender discussion of her and his desire to destroy the Intersect, the guard rail disappears.

A scene presenting Chuck in "vs. Imported Hard Salami" echoes this approach. When Chuck grows suspicious that Lou is in league with her ex-boyfriend Stavros importing contraband at the docks at the harbor, he follows her to observe their transaction. The camera proceeds to present the exchange between Lou and Stavros from Chuck's point of view as he hides behind perforated mats that hang over a railing, achieving an effect similar to Sarah's peering through the guard rail and figuring Chuck's skepticism of Lou's actions. When he finally confronts Lou, however, Chuck finds her guilty of only petty crime: smuggling Portuguese cured sopresseto.

Yet another pair of scenes, both opening their respective seasons, present a spiraling camera angle that includes metaphorical overtones. "Vs. First Date" begins Season 2 with a scene in which Chuck initially appears to be upright, only to have the lens circle 180 degrees while panning backward and upward. Soon, the viewer realizes that Chuck is actually being held upside down off the edge of a high-rise by Mr. Colt. Like the camera panning back, the viewer comes to see the full significance of this special effect only when viewing the scene in the larger context of the full episode and even season. Indeed, though Chuck ended Season 1 and begins Season 2 on the verge of a real relationship with Sarah and a return to civilian life, that paradigm is soon turned upside down, first with a pending assassination order and second by an uncertain future when the new Intersect is destroyed and the order rescinded. In fact, Chuck will spend most of Season 2 trying to get the Intersect out of his head and achieve normalcy. Given that perspective, one realizes that the opening camera sequence foreshadows Chuck's spy life will spiral out of control and invert his life just when he thought it was manageable.

The opening scene of Season 4 reverses the direction of the lens' spiral. As Mary Bartowski reads a young Chuck a bedtime story, the frame opens by holding the two upside down, only to return to an upright position by the time it stops spinning. As with the prior example, this special effect foreshadows the events of the entire season. Whereas Chuck and Ellie begin the season estranged from their spy mother, who is also thought to have gone rogue, matters are ultimately set aright: the reunited family finds healing, and Frost is vindicated as an agent.

Aside from the elements of cinematography found in "Chuck", a variety of stage props also add texture to the visual text. Among these, the use of the flat screens in the Buy More proves the most consistently utilized. Indeed, almost every episode includes projections in the background that metaphorically accent the surface action. Consequently, the analysis here must be limited to some of the more memorable instances.

Many of the images pertain to particular characters and the specific situation they face. As noted in Chapter 1, Chuck's baptism into the hazardous and obstacle-filled spy life finds expression through underwater and off-roading footage in the series' first two episodes. Similarly, Jeff's emergence from a mostly moronic, immoral soul lacking a work ethic into a model of insight, discipline and virtue is imaged by spring greenery and blossoms when he first walks back into the Buy More (vs. Frosted Tips). Morgan takes his turn, too, though the message is not so inspiring. In the episode after he is admitted into Chuck's spy life (vs. Tic Tac), Morgan, code name Cobra, has already shown pathetic signs of imitating a romanticized and stereotypical spy but lacks the natural abilities to actually be one. Desperate to act out his imitation identity, he is duped by the rogue Casey to retrieve the Laudanol from the "Planet of the Apes" DVD at the Buy More in which he had hidden it. Playing on the definition of "ape" as a verb meaning to imitate, the flat screens surrounding Morgan project images of apes when he is apprehended by Chuck, also accenting the DVD selection.

Other flat screen images target pairs of characters. The farewell of Jeffster as they leave the Buy More for fame and fortune in Germany is accented by footage of cowboys riding off into the sunset (vs. Goodbye). Other cases prove satirical, with Chuck and Sarah's strange romance serving as fodder. Prior to and during their awkward discussion of how to spend Valentine's Day evening, which ends with their greedily accepting a mission to escape silently sitting on opposite ends of a couch, the flat screens project scenes from "Must Love Dogs", a romantic comedy (vs. Suburbs). The movie chronicles a problematic romance featuring a woman named Sarah who finally communicates her feelings for her lover at the end of the movie. The fact that they met at a dog park possibly adds commentary on the Buy More Nerd Herders!

Chuck and Jill's romance receives the same treatment. Chapter 5 details the influence of "La Traviata" on the Jill arc, which links their relationship with the opera. In parody, the flat screens project scenes from "What's Opera, Doc?", the classic Warner Bros. cartoon starring a balletic Bugs Bunny and Elmer Fudd. Clearly, the comic comparison is not a flattering one.

This cursory overview could extend to cover additional special effects, including the use of dark-filtered photography discussed elsewhere (See Chapter 14: Sarah vs. Sarah and *Unpacking "Chuck"* Chapter 14: Phase Three). Likewise, most stage props have been omitted here, though noted in analysis throughout both books. Of these, the variety of baptism-related items, ranging from fire sprinklers and showers to fountains, oceans, and pitchers of water, show vivid imagination, as does the inclusion of time-related devices. Still, what has been addressed is sufficient to demonstrate that, along with the use of hand props, the visual text of "Chuck" is a layered one requiring viewers to pay close attention to glean its full meaning.

Chapter 11: Shaw - Windsor Night

Part I: Snapping Shut

What's in a name?
A rose by any other name would smell as sweet.

Romeo and Juliet, seeing no intrinsic value in their family names, proved ready to toss them aside as meaningless labels in exchange for the more substantial pledge of their love for one another. In the case of CIA Special Agent Daniel Shaw, however, the name is far more indelibly linked to the substance it labels.

In one regard, Shaw's surname derives from the English word for "copse" or "thicket", an apt title for one who remains shrouded in mystery for much of his tenure, especially at the outset. Indeed, in his first appearance (vs. Three Words), during which he sits on the edge of Beckman's desk in D. C., the audience is allowed only a partial view of the silent master spy, his face hidden outside the frame. Moreover, his only action in the scene, a symbolic one, consists of snapping shut the lid of a cigarette lighter he tumbles with his fingers. Notably, the same sharp closing action using the lighter, foregrounded by the lens, announces his initial appearance in Castle, despite the fact that he doesn't smoke (vs. Operation Awesome). Thus, Shaw is metaphorically introduced to viewers as an enigmatic figure who not only nurses a burning passion but keeps his emotions and purposes closed off from the view of others (vs. First Class).

The tight lid Shaw keeps on affairs immediately evidences itself before he leaves Beckman's office (vs. Three Words). The NSA general urges the CIA agent, "We can't keep this a secret any more…We need to tell [the Castle agents]. They need to be prepared." But Shaw doesn't heed Beckman's plea. In an undisclosed "set-up", he arranges for Chuck and

Devon to meet him in his twelfth floor CIA office without his surprised handlers, Sarah and Casey, who find themselves locked in the van under orders to "stand down" (vs. Operation Awesome). Similarly, when he directs Chuck's first solo mission from Castle, Shaw reveals to Chuck that the mark is actually on the plane, not in Paris as he had been told, and even then only after he has flashed on Panzer in mid-flight (vs. First Class).

Observing this ambush, Sarah turns to their new boss and pointedly asks, "Who are you, Agent Shaw? Because I have never heard of you, and neither has Casey." And when Agent Walker adds, "You're a very well-kept secret," he candidly replies, "I do like my secrets." Chuck, however, is actually the first to ask the question. Upon reaching Shaw's high-rise CIA office with Devon in tow, Chuck is taken aback not only by Shaw's anticipation of his arrival, but also by Shaw's subsequent instructions to put the gun in Devon's hand and read the contents of an envelope after Chuck shoots him in the heart (vs. Operation Awesome). By the time Shaw is ready to have the trigger pulled, Chuck, with puzzled eyes, muses, "Who are you?" Further driving the point home, Serena, the astonished Ring agent on board the airliner mission, asks the question yet again when speaking to Shaw on speaker phone in the cargo hold: "Who are you?" (vs. First Class).

The answer to this fundamental question of identity progressively reveals itself over the next two plus years. From the beginning, though, Shaw is invested with such superhuman traits that the title of the episode, "vs. Operation Awesome", likely refers as much to the CIA special agent as it does to Devon. The moment he meets Chuck in the 12th floor office, Shaw immediately claims an almost divine omniscience. After stunning the Intersect by voicing Chuck's full name, the stranger continues, "I know things, lots of things, about you, about [The Ring]," including the imminent arrival of Sidney, The Ring agent. Of course, the man who sports an Annapolis t-shirt (vs. First Class) and boasts a West Point transcript in his file (vs. Other Guy) also concocts a shrewdly dangerous plan to convince The Ring and their attractive operative that he no longer lives.

Shaw doubles down on his claim of supreme knowledge when the Castle team finally meets their new boss (vs. Operation Awesome). After telling the agents that he has been fully briefed on the details of the Intersect, The Ring expert insists, "I know everything," and he consistently backs up his claim. Acknowledging Sarah's status as "the daughter of a con man" earns him her back-handed compliment: "You really do read everyone's files" (vs. First Class). Even those of the Buy More staff, it turns out. When Chuck hesitates in obeying Shaw's orders to practice his tranqing skills by spiking Jeff's coffee, his new boss assures him, "I've read everyone's file. Jeff Barnes will be just fine." To the shock of Serena, The Ring agent on Chuck's flight, Shaw knows not only her name but where the toxin with which Chuck has been poisoned was last used.

But Shaw's insight particularly returns to focus itself on Sarah. When not startling her with questions regarding her off-grid movements around Prague and Lisbon in prior months, which he guesses may have had something to do with Chuck (vs. First Class), he stirs up matters by bringing Sarah her favorite coffee blend ("double shot Café Americano") and noting her nervous habit of chewing on swizzle sticks (vs. Mask).

In addition to his seeming omniscience, the CIA version of God demonstrates an impressive degree of omnipotence. Casey makes it clear that, given his status as a special agent, their new boss "can pretty much do whatever he wants" (vs. First Class). General Beckman echoes this point when informing Team Bartowski, "From this point forward, Agent Shaw has complete command authority over any mission having to do with The Ring" (vs. Operation Awesome). In fact, Shaw's faceless debut, in which he feels free to lounge on her desk and stroll away while ignoring her pleas, leaves even the general appearing subordinate. Chuck soon personally discovers the extent of Shaw's control—and willingness to use it—when admonished by him during a meeting to discuss the Intersect. Uncomfortable with the silence, the spy-in-training takes the initiative to break the ice only to be silenced by Shaw: "Chuck, this is my meeting." And when Sarah in the same meeting voices her concerns about Chuck's preparedness for a solo mission, Shaw summarily declares, "Duly noted...and ignored."

An implied omnipresence and perfection accent these theistic traits. While Shaw takes control of the aircraft, via satellite, to bail out a poisoned Chuck on his mid-flight mission (vs. First Class), he corrects the gloating Ring agent by informing her, "My people are never alone," and later adds to Sarah, "I do everything I can to protect my people." Part of the wonder of the feat is the fact that the pilots will "never even know we were there." Regarding this same mission, Shaw also insists, "I'm right, aren't I? I should tell you that I'm always right. Annoying but true." Not quite finished, he goes on to tell Agent Walker, "I was right about this mission, and I'm right about you," challenging Sarah's instinct to protect and not push Chuck.

If these divine traits don't grab the audience's attention, the specifically Christological ones that complement them serve as an exclamation point. It's hard to ignore the fact that Shaw resurrects from the dead in his first talking scene of the series, even if he does receive assists from the Amiodarone and Dr. Woodcomb (vs. Operation Awesome). Is it surprising, then, when the Resurrection Man later gently chides Casey's skepticism of a decision he makes by stating, "Ye of little faith"? In this context, the repeated questions regarding the identity of the seeming miracle-worker, noted above, further link him to a messianic ministry.

Shaw certainly attempts to disciple his Castle charges, particularly Chuck and Sarah, turning the episode title presenting Chuck's airplane mission, "vs. First Class", into a double entendre. From the start, Shaw tries to raise Chuck's performance to help the asset reach his dream of becoming an official spy. Diagnosing the fundamental flaw as the "coddling" of his handlers (vs. First Class), Shaw urges Chuck to become less dependent on Sarah and Casey, who won't let him "evolve". Assuring Chuck he can be a "great spy," Shaw begins training him in spy craft with the tranq pen and encourages him to take his first solo mission: "Listen, you've been on more missions [in two years] than most spies in a lifetime. Trust me: you're ready." And even before Chuck's impressive turn as Rafe the assassin (vs. Fake Name), Shaw the cheerleader claims the Intersect is "performing. He can do this. He's ready…." Thus, when his prophecy comes true on the mission, with Chuck shrewdly and boldly saving Casey's life, it leads to Shaw's broadly smiling praise: "Listen to him. He's completely living the lie." Likewise, before his final exam, the Red Test, Shaw asserts that Chuck "can do this. You can pass this test. It's everything you've been working toward" (vs. Final Exam). When a fooled Sarah reports that he passed the test, another smile fills the face of Shaw, proud of his pupil, while he proclaims, "Chuck is a spy." Alternatively, when Shaw realizes Chuck hasn't flashed in a week, he protects him and others by benching him, explaining, "Off nights get agents killed" (vs. Beard).

Shaw tries to teach the seasoned Agent Walker a few spy lessons, too. When Sarah instinctively moves to answer Chuck's call from the plane on the Panzer mission, the spy mentor ironically warns, "Go ahead, answer it. Just know that if you do, he'll never be a real spy. One day that will get him killed" (vs. First Class). Similarly, while Sarah laments Chuck's passing of the Red Test, Shaw reaffirms that Chuck did it for the same greater good they all do: "to serve his country," continuing, "It's never easy, but it helps to save lives. Never forget that" (vs. Final Exam). Even while on the verge of exiting Castle to face his likely death from a bunker busting bomb, Sarah's erstwhile lover has a parting word of exhortation: "Hey, we're spies, Walker. Let's start acting like one" (vs. American Hero).

When not discipling his agents, Shaw saves them, beginning with his requisite death the night he first meets Chuck. With Sidney moments away from his office, the Resurrection Man informs the Intersect, "If you don't kill me now, you and Devon are as good as dead...There's no other way" (vs. Operation Awesome). After Chuck still proves unable to pull the trigger, Shaw does so on Chuck's behalf. At the end of the very same episode, Shaw also shoots Sidney, who has Chuck dead to rights, graciously reneging on his vow to have Chuck finish what he starts. Of course, Chuck will later repay the favor more than once. Shaw later saves Sarah, too, carrying her from Castle to the museum when it would have taken too long for the antidote to reach them (vs. Mask).

However, Shaw's supreme expression of selflessness comes when he voluntarily offers up his life to take out The Ring leadership (vs. American Hero). Just in case the viewer isn't cluing back into the Christological motif, Sarah explains to Chuck, "He's sacrificing himself." An exceedingly painful process, it involves having a sizable satellite tracker forcibly removed from his digestive tract, his notably outstretched arms held by Ring operatives while he writhes in agony, not long after he somehow manages to swallow it. Earlier in the same episode, Shaw himself jokes that the corpse from which a similar object is retracted is "lucky he was dead first." Additional words and deeds also specifically imitate The Crucifixion. Shaw's solemn acknowledgment, "It's done," after placing the call to The Ring echoes Christ's last words spoken on the cross, "It is finished," just as his last directive to Chuck concerning Sarah, "Take care of her," mirrors Jesus' final instructions to his disciple John regarding his mother, Mary.

To these divine traits, the text adds another layer of singular characteristics portraying Shaw as 'merely' an earth-bound, "Supermanny kind of guy" (vs. Mask). Even Chuck's best friend defines the special agent as "handsome, worldly and know[ing] his way around a menu" (vs. American Hero). If the point isn't clear enough, both Casey and Morgan, on separate occasions, call Shaw "a real stallion", just as Morgan and Jeff notice he can "fill out a pair of slacks." Earlier, Hannah, doe-eyed for Chuck, spots Shaw on the museum surveillance camera and still considers him "ridiculously good looking" (vs. Mask). And when a tongue-tied Sarah drops in on her nonchalant, towel-clad boss in "vs. Fake Name", her visible distraction leads to an embarrassed request for him to put some clothes on…minutes before embracing him.

Perhaps emboldened by his looks, Shaw displays an uncanny self-confidence in pursuing romantic interests. The Ring specialist proves unintimidated by the grenades Sarah lobs his way to prevent his advances at the beginning of their relationship. Whether suffering through Agent Walker's chastisement for bringing her coffee, for asking about the sexual dynamics of their cover prior to the museum mission, or for wrapping his arm around her on that mission, he accepts each rebuke with a chuckle and a grin (vs. Mask). In the last case, he actually admonishes Sarah for acting like they're at a "middle school dance" and brashly proceeds to apply his lips to her neck, leaving Sarah stunned. Moreover, he possesses the self-assuredness to admit, "I'd be a liar if I didn't say I was disappointed…," to a still-balking Sarah after her "pre-emptive breakup" (vs. Fake Name).

In concert with the shift in the complex dynamics of Sarah's relationship with Chuck and, consequently, her own existential crisis, Shaw's persistence in battering down Agent Walker's defensive walls is ultimately rewarded when the one who formerly despised him in public transforms into a docile, tongue-tied dame willing to throw her lot in with him in the privacy of his hotel room. Indeed, with his insistent coaxing, Sarah feels compelled to reveal one significant secret her boss cannot find in her file: her real name. Devon, an expert on self-confidence himself, perhaps best summarizes Shaw after observing him lead Sarah into the restaurant and order for her the night before they are slated to leave for D.C. together: "That's a power move, Bro" (vs. American Hero). Even Casey, no fan, adds, "The guy's a closer."

Shaw's self-confident pursuit of Sarah is partly the product of his sexual assuredness. Indeed, the matter is on his mind from the beginning of his career in Castle. When Sarah admits that the Intersect is not able to "perform" when he panics, Shaw retorts with a pun: "Yeah, it happens to lots of guys…or so I hear" (vs. Operation Awesome). The same mindset lurks behind the sexual questions he asks Agent Walker about their museum mission cover. Not surprisingly, the man who owns a copy of *The Guide to Getting It On* and the *Karma Sutra* (vs. Living Dead) isn't afraid to tell Sarah he wants to eat her dessert over lunch either, or compliment her for persisting in the impersonal use of his last name, calling it "very sexy" (vs. Fake Name). Soon, Sarah is sharing a couples' massage in D.C. (when not purchasing Tiffany diamond ear rings) and afternoons in his downtown loft (vs. Living Dead). As Sarah herself tells Chuck, the sensually-oriented spy romance she shares with her emotionally-closed boss "is different" than the Platonic one she and Chuck enjoyed (vs. Final Exam / For more on Shaw's relationship with Sarah, see *Unpacking Chuck* Chapter 12: Wandering into the Promised Land).

But the hunk possesses a variety of moral virtues to complement his physical ones as well. Perhaps the product of his reading *Zen Buddhism: A History* (vs. Living Dead), Shaw deals with emergencies by displaying impressively courageous calm. The poise he demonstrates when shooting himself in the heart, especially when depending on a wobbly Chuck to save him, bears note. Later, finding himself stuck in the museum vault trying to switch out the mask before the exhibit opens, and consequently suffocating to death, the special agent simply shrugs before calling Casey to blandly inquire whether "the Intersect isn't busy" (vs. Mask). Likewise, when Castle is contaminated with the lethal gas from the mask, Shaw retains the presence of mind, even in his debilitated state, to take Sarah and himself to the antidote, knowing it will be too late if he does not. No hesitation or doubts surface while "painting a target" for the Stealth bomber either, and while on that mission, he twice collectedly tells Ring operatives, "If you're going to kill me, get it over with."

Shaw also doesn't let emotions interfere when dealing with Chuck, ultimately his rival for Sarah. In the midst of their pseudo-brawl over Sarah at Shaw's hotel room during the Rafe assassin episode, Shaw, with dramatic irony, claims, "You had your chance…and you blew it" (vs. Fake Name). However, the Castle boss checks his feelings at the door while making professional decisions regarding the Intersect. When The Ring agents penetrate Castle and seize Chuck, Shaw is faced with the decision over whether to activate the self-destruct mechanism (vs. Beard). Knowing full well that the rogue agents busy themselves with accessing "every piece of intelligence we have," he could legitimately and immediately order the compound's—and thus Chuck's—elimination. Instead, resisting any jealous or vengeful temptation he might harbor towards Chuck, Shaw honors Sarah's ostensible appeal to his sense of loyalty for the honorable service of a spy team member. Though he may well have sensed an ulterior motive in her request, he nevertheless grants a five-minute delay. Those five extra minutes provide Chuck enough time to free Morgan and himself. Shaw also shows reason and restraint, though still taking a risk, when allowing Morgan into the Castle Club rather than remand him to a witness protection program, accepting Chuck's (and Sarah's) argument that Morgan is needed to stabilize the Intersect emotionally and get him performing.

Finally, Shaw evidences patience and even humor with inconvenient or irritating situations that others might very well deal with using a more heavy hand. When the Buy Morons stage a revolutionary blockade to prevent the alleged sale of the store, Castle's chief executive, using an accent no less, calls from "Buy More corporate" to inform Big Mike that, impressed with the "most incredible display of store loyalty," the decision has been made to rescind the closure (vs. Beard). Similarly, Shaw good-naturedly shrugs off the efforts of Team Bartowski to prevent his leaving town with Sarah on the eve of their departure for D.C. After tracking Morgan's distorted cell phone call, he simply and gently apologizes to the Bearded One before using him as a Taser shield. When Awesome tackles him through the restaurant window soon thereafter, he even manages to crack a joke: "Next time, tackle the guy with the gun" (vs. American Hero).

Despite his superhuman qualities, though, Shaw still has an Achilles' Heel. For a while, as imaged during his introduction by the repeated closing of the cigarette lighter, The Ring expert keeps a fiery passion shut off from the prying eyes of others. Shaw hints at the truth when trying to teach Chuck and Sarah another lesson: "Family and friends make us vulnerable" (vs. Operation Awesome). By the end of that episode, his meaning becomes a bit clearer. Alone in Castle, Shaw stares at a ring he pulls out of its case and slips it on his wedding finger while watching the surveillance feed of the family dinner at Chuck's attended by Team Bartowski. In the next episode (vs. First Class), the lid cracks open a tad more when Shaw admits, with a hint of self-loathing, that he "lost one spy. It was my fault. And it will never happen again."

However, when his deceased wife's spy will finally ends up in Castle, the veil obscuring his obsessive motivation for pursuing The Ring is pulled off completely. At first none of his Castle colleagues knows the identity of the agent whose will they unlock, only that the lock box, from "an agent I had inside the Ring," contains "all the intel the agent had" and will give them "a chance" against the rogue organization. But when Shaw leaves for his office with an envelope from the lock box that he intends to read privately, Sarah follows him to ask about it. Silently, Shaw responds by handing him a woman's wedding ring set, followed by a blunt revelation: "She was killed by a Ring agent five years ago. Her name was Evelyn Shaw. Eve." Speechless, Sarah withdraws from the room, but not before her boss leaves her with one last thought: "We both made the same mistake, Sarah: we fell in love with spies," referring to Sarah's trip to Lisbon to scatter the ashes of Bryce Larkin.

Is it any wonder, then, that Shaw, when "the moment [he's] been waiting for" presents itself "to decimate The Ring's command structure with a single mission," proves ready to "trade my life for the man who killed my wife"? (vs. American Hero). Betraying a compulsion to match his obsession, Shaw turns to Sarah, whom he brushes aside as if an afterthought, and explains, "I have to do this; I'm sorry." The lens later focuses on Shaw donning his wedding ring when leaving the hospital in search of Sarah and again when driving through the desert at the episode's conclusion, his intent "to settle an old score." This obsession is further confirmed when the sacrificial lamb shows up at the bunker beneath the empty warehouse, where he finds a holographic version of The Ring director greeting him with the news of "a gift...the answer you've been seeking all these years": the identity of the one who killed his wife.

Nothing could prepare him for the emotional blow of that "gift". At just the sight of his wife, smiling and waving at him on the banks of screens surrounding him, Shaw, with welling eyes and unhinged mouth, comes undone. When the footage transitions to the night of her death, and the shots are fired into his wife's body, Shaw involuntarily jerks as if he himself has been shot. When the video ultimately reveals Sarah as the perpetrator of the deed, Shaw, in decidedly un-Shaw-like manner, fragments internally into as many pieces as there are separate screens projecting the truth while he screams and lunges to strike the phantom image of the Director. Within this context, Shaw's snapping the cigarette lighter shut in his debut scenes serves as the foreshadowing of his ultimate psychological lock down cued by his flaming obsession. A compulsive withdrawal into the moral night of misguided revenge follows.

Let there be no mistake: Shaw at this moment experiences a dark rebirth ironically announced by none other than his wife, who calls out to him from the video screens, "Happy Birthday!" Accordingly, the lens prominently frames him twice with a French traffic yield sign ("Cedez Le Passage") while he stands with Sarah on the Paris sidewalk where his wife died. Even so, he yields to his craving for retribution in a dubious effort to alleviate his devastating loss, telling Sarah, "You killed my wife. Did you really think I'd be OK with that?" (vs. Other Guy).

However, Shaw's compulsion extends beyond a mere personal vendetta. As The Ring director explains, Shaw also nourishes a new desire "not only [to] avenge his wife's death but...destroy the very institution that ordered her murder: your CIA." Shaw himself elaborates, "I'm going to send a message to the CIA that they betrayed the wrong man...They need to feel the pain that I felt." The images of dramatic change noted above are accented by the final image of Shaw in the initial arc. As he loses his grip on Sarah's wrist, dangling from the bridge over the Seine, it also implies the loss of Shaw's psychological grip, and the once-glorious husband of Eve falls into the black, frigid waters, his dark baptism complete.

And he does lose the grip on his psyche. In the aftermath of Shaw's discovering his wife's killer, Chuck describes him as both "an emotional train wreck" and psychological "Swiss cheese" (vs. Other Guy). Indeed, one can drive a truck through the holes in his delusional reasoning. In the desert warehouse, Shaw himself acknowledges, "They used you; they manipulated you. You had no idea that the Ring was behind this...This isn't your fault." Similarly, The Ring director exonerates Sarah: "You're boss, Langston Graham, assigned you to kill her. You did what you were told." Despite these testimonies, Shaw still rationalizes, "I have to kill you," simply because of the pain he feels. In contrast, Shaw displays no compulsion to kill Chuck, his former romantic rival, even after he initially foils the Intersect's attempt to save Sarah, though he warns that will change if Chuck pursues the matter further.

Moreover, Sarah's former lover displays not only a "morbid sentimentality" but also a bizarre, irrational concept of intimacy and compassion detached from reality. The one who visited Paris every year in memory of Eve's death also yearns to share the view of the river with Sarah prior to killing her, deriving meaning from the gesture because "it's beautiful at night." Similarly, Shaw, fancying himself humane, assures Sarah that she "won't feel a thing" when he kills her due to the toxin immobilizing her.

Chuck, following his unhinged boss to the bridge, attempts to reach him yet. Lowering his pistol, the Intersect asserts, "This isn't you, Shaw. You can't do this." Shaw hesitates, pondering Chuck's words. It seems for a moment that they penetrate, and he appears on the verge of relenting. But then the flashbacks come. With each gunshot he relives in his mind, the resolve of Eve's husband stiffens until he issues a final answer: "No Chuck, I can. You can't." Alas, the human cigarette lighter snaps shut for good, succumbing to his burning and misplaced passion; an obsession that will continue to burn when the Resurrection Man is resurrected yet again.

CHAPTER 12: SHAW - WINDSOR NIGHT

Part II: Wolf In Sheep's Clothing

What's in a name? In the case of CIA Special Agent Daniel Shaw, perhaps even more substance than one might initially suspect. As discussed in the last chapter, his surname can be traced to the English word for copse or thicket, appropriate given The Ring expert's proclivity for hiding a burning passion for revenge, accented by the imagery of his repeated snapping a cigarette lighter shut. In an etymological curiosity, however, the surname is alternatively derived from the Gaelic word for "wolf". This latter meaning, particularly when viewed in concert with the Christological imagery that figures Shaw and his role as shepherd of the flock of Castle agents he disciples, implies that Shaw spends the second half of his tenure in the series acting as a wolf in sheep's clothing. Indeed, he continues to give the outward appearance of virtue even after his dark baptism while hiding his sustained, misguided desire to avenge his wife's death.

This reading of the audio-visual text certainly bears out during Shaw's stalking of Sarah at the end of the initial arc. When the American Hero arrives at Sarah's hotel room, allegedly to follow the scent of "a trace on The [Ring] director" (vs. American Hero), he really takes her to the desert, a nod to the moral wilderness which Shaw now inhabits, to "settle an old score" with her. Once they arrive (vs. Other Guy), Shaw lets Agent Walker take the lead and discover the horrifying footage of her Red Test alone. As he follows, though, his gun drawn, he takes a lengthy bead on his former lover as he slowly approaches her. But just as Shaw prepares to pounce on his prey, his eyes subtly dart in the direction away from the screens, toward the area from which Chuck and his squad will appear, and then back to Sarah, the muzzle of his gun suddenly lifted. Apparently alerted to their approach, the master spy coolly shifts gears in an instant and leaves his sheep-like facade in place without betraying his evil intent or the knowledge that they have been followed.

In fact, he suddenly becomes a paragon of tenderness and understanding. Though Shaw softly encourages Sarah, "Just take a breath," the words primarily apply to him, for the raw emotion of his narrowly averted attack leaves his chest visibly heaving. From there he pleads Sarah's case of ignorance for her, and they even embrace, with Sarah ironically placing her head on the predator's shoulder. Thus, when Chuck and company find the couple, they stand before a makeshift stage, the backdrop figuring the fact that The Wolf's impromptu, compassionate response is a staged event. Accordingly, Chuck will later discover that "the fight was staged" in which Shaw takes out the operatives above the elevator shaft during the subsequent mission to apprehend The Ring director. What makes the "fake action sequence" additionally intriguing is the context in which it occurs: Shaw claims to be tapping into The Ring's "internal security system" when 'attacked', suggesting Shaw's fakery actually stems from the penetration of his own inner defense mechanisms.

But Shaw's turn as a sheep is only in its first act. Subsequently, he puts on another counterfeit performance in the Castle briefing session that follows the desert warehouse scene and during which the human thicket subtly obscures the truth. After finishing Chuck's thought about Shaw's betraying his country in a non-declarative manner, Shaw ironically defends Chuck, who has just been chastised by Beckman over the excesses of his rescue effort, for "looking out for his partner and the agency," adding, "I would have done the same." Smoothly, Shaw even manages to follow up with some humor to put his colleagues at ease: "Maybe without the stealth bombers, but perhaps that's just me." From there, The Wolf masks his intentions with dramatic irony, claiming, "This isn't the first time that they've used one of our own against us," meaning himself as much as Sarah's shooting of Eve five years prior. And truer words were never spoken when Shaw continues, "I want to make sure it's the last." Only then does Shaw resort to an outright lie. Affirming he can continue to work with Agent Walker, he asserts, "We both want the same thing: to capture the Director and take down The Ring," before directly appealing to her. In the middle of this act, however, Shaw sneaks in a key question: who ordered Sarah's Red Test on Evelyn Shaw? When

Beckman replies that Langston Graham "took the secret to his grave," it seemingly scratches one person off Shaw's revenge list.

Notably, Shaw fools everyone with his benevolent performance. Before the traitor pulls off another staged event, the execution of The Ring director, which also includes the pseudo fight, Chuck privately voices his concerns to Beckman. When suggesting, "Nobody can control their feelings that well," the general replies, "Chuck, what you are seeing in Shaw is an absolute professional, something you are not." Likewise, after Chuck shares his misgivings to Sarah, she responds with confidence in their boss: "Shaw is one step closer to capturing the Director. And I'm sure that is all he is thinking about, so don't even worry." Ultimately, even Chuck is taken in. Prior to showing Morgan footage of the faux fight sequence, the Intersect confesses, "I may have said some unfortunate things about Shaw, but the fact of the matter is the guy is exactly what he seems: a hero."

Thus, Sarah departs with Shaw for Paris, alone. To create the opportunity for his "morbid[ly]" sentimental revenge, Shaw apparently fabricates the need to travel to France, the location where the components of the Cypher for the new Intersect were allegedly and pointedly "fabricated". When Shaw also cites a number of problems with the Cypher, the scenario takes on added metaphorical meaning: not only is the Cypher an ironic figure for Shaw's own twisted mind, beyond decoding, but the supposed location of its design parallels the site of the event, his wife's death, responsible for manufacturing Shaw's vengeful malice. Only when an already drugged Sarah finally realizes the elaborate thicket in which she has been trapped does The Wolf finally discard his woolen disguise, candidly admitting, "I did a lot of things to get you here." Thankfully, Chuck's instinct, research, and newfound resolve to pull the trigger prevent Shaw from devouring his prey.

That doesn't mean Shaw permanently discards his costume. Indeed, when he resurrects for a second time and returns at the end of Season 3, the wolf-in-sheep's-clothing metaphor still applies even if the target of his revenge and ultimate purposes evidence some alteration.

With or without the Intersect, Shaw 2.0 still evidences many of the same traits observed in his initial advent. The Wolf proves clever as a fox, concocting a shrewd alibi for his treachery and plan still to achieve it. After claiming to have worked as a double agent within The Ring, creating a word-against-word scenario, Shaw undermines Chuck's credibility while enhancing his own. First, Shaw shows signs of seeming omniscience when calling the original Intersect an "American hero" who, as a result of taking on a burden not of his own choosing, suffers a deteriorating mind due to the long-term effects of the Intersect. Of course, Chuck hasn't told even Sarah the full truth of Dr. Dreyfuss' final, classified report. Shaw also conveys a faux humaneness when conjuring up sympathy for Chuck by alleging his understanding of Chuck's desire not to worry Sarah about his condition. Moreover, when Chuck makes the accusation that he saw Shaw flash and is therefore an Intersect, Shaw smartly refrains from reacting to the letter opener Chuck hurls at his rival, despite the injury he receives, thereby enhancing his claim of Chuck's progressing insanity. Even later, when preparing to execute the Castle Crew after carting them away in the armored truck, Shaw first gives them keys to uncuff themselves so that when he executes them it will appear they were trying to escape.

Shaw also slyly succeeds in manipulating both Chuck and Sarah when he gets them to step into his baited traps. By tapping boldly on the subway car window, revealing that he remains among the living, he sets in motion a chain of events that logically ends with Team Bartowski crashing the secret intelligence summit and giving him the platform he needs to discredit Chuck. Similarly, by later arresting Sarah, Shaw draws Chuck and Orion back into town. Though the sequence of events doesn't transpire exactly the way Shaw envisioned when the Bartowskis penetrate the secret Ring base in the subway, it still ends with Chuck's capture after Shaw has boasted, "This time I'll be ready for them."

On the other hand, Sarah takes the bait in Shaw's office soon after he secretly pushes an emergency button under his desk (vs. Subway). Goaded into an emotional response she cannot suppress, when he mocks Chuck's mental condition and abuses the intimate revelation of her real name, Agent Walker pulls her gun on Shaw...just in time for the responding security personnel to see and Shaw to proclaim prophetically, "Knew you'd bite." In contrast, Shaw will not take the bait Chuck offers in the subway: instead of biting on his taunt to come take the governor off his wrist himself, his former boss assigns the task to another while he keeps Chuck at gunpoint. And Shaw won't be coaxed into an Intersect vs. Intersect fight either, at least not unless Chuck is first emotionally disabled by the sight of his father's murder.

Shaw 2.0 proves the same old Shaw in other ways, too. Agent Walker's sexually-oriented boss greets her in his office by noting, "I'd be remiss if I didn't say you look great, Walker" (vs. Subway), and Shaw hasn't developed a shred of self-doubt. When Casey, languishing in a detention cell with Sarah, asserts he's not going to get away with his plot, Shaw, without hesitation, replies, "Yes, I will." Shaw hasn't lost any of his Zen approach either: controlling his reaction to Chuck's throwing of the letter opener is no small feat, and he offers no response to Sarah's final blow to his head upon her goaded arrest other than a grin. Even news of the Bartowski's infiltration of The Ring's subway base yields only a quiet, expressionless "dammit" before Shaw turns to deal with it.

However, Shaw, having receded deeper into the depths of his dark baptism, does bring a new, cruel mockery to accent his arrogance. Besides smirking with feigned compassion over Chuck's serious psychological condition, Shaw clearly enjoys his abuse of Sarah's name in his office. Moreover, dripping with condescension and perhaps driven by jealousy, Shaw lambasts "Sam" with fake disappointment over the change Chuck has wrought in her life: "It's a shame. I remember when nothing affected you. Now you're as emotional as your boyfriend." When the Castle Crew is being carted away for execution, he ridicules Chuck's despondency, "Love the new defeatist attitude, Chuck," before glibly encouraging them to "enjoy this ride together [and] bond. Share war stories, because as soon as the truck stops, so do your lives." Most notably, though, Shaw not only executes Orion in front of Chuck's eyes but then smirks at the son while asking, "How you feeling now?"

Another element that changes in Shaw's second advent is the target of his wrath and the purpose of his actions. Though Shaw still wishes to destroy Sarah, he also wants to kill Chuck, who foiled him in Paris. Attempting to hit two birds with one stone, he plans to deprive Sarah of Chuck, just as she allegedly deprived him of Eve, so she will feel the full brunt of the pain he experiences. Also, Shaw no longer simply wishes to "send a message to the CIA" as an institution (vs. Other Guy), but take it over and replace General Beckman on the Joint Security Summit. However, he also wants to download into his brain the very Intersect that he himself has aided The Ring to complete with the files he traitorously handed to the Director when betraying Sarah in Paris. To do that safely, though, he needs the 2.0 governor Orion has made for Chuck, which gives him a double incentive for taking out Chuck.

As masterfully crafted as Shaw's plan to take over the CIA and indulge his passion for revenge is, Team Bartowski succeeds in exposing The Wolf in sheep's clothing a second time. Initially, the Zen Master remains composed when receiving Chuck's phone call in the middle of his address to the security summit (vs. Ring Part II), excusing himself from the stage and then standing calmly with folded arms in his own office, where he meets Chuck. But the seemingly omniscient one is soon shown the limits of his knowledge when outwitted with relative ease by his "Nerd Herd associate." After Casey and Morgan corral the Ring elders, notified by Shaw to leave the building before he exits the stage, Chuck succeeds in getting Shaw to implicate himself to a live audience via a laptop video conference. When Sarah saves her short-circuiting boyfriend, Shaw, trading places with Chuck as the fugitive, escapes. However, the lens again images how severely the traitorous Shaw has turned from virtue to evil, for the one portrayed as "Supermanny" in the initial arc pointedly reprises a Super Man scene when using the American flag to swing 180 degrees before crashing through another office window.

The dynamic remains the same in the climactic series of events at the Buy More. Shaw first wires the Buy More for detonation to lure Chuck out of Castle for a final confrontation. The new Intersect then begins the epic encounter against the original, short-circuiting Intersect with a semblance of chivalry, lowering his gun along with Chuck when accepting the challenge. When the tide against a rebooted Chuck turns against him, though, Shaw reaches for the detonator, preferring to blow up all three of them, including Sarah, than realize defeat. And when Chuck holds him in a death grip by the throat reminiscent of Chuck's hold on another villain in "vs. Tic Tac", Shaw clutches at the only straw left: to change Chuck into a person that he never wanted to be and one that Sarah could no longer love. "You have to do it. You have to kill me," he manages to choke out, and when a wiser Chuck refuses to take the bait and releases him, Shaw claims his inability to kill makes him "weak." Sarah begs to differ. After gaining her own bit of revenge by vigorously applying a metal pipe to the back of Shaw's head, she corrects The Wolf: "No! That's what makes you great!"

By the time Shaw appears in his final advent almost two years later (vs. Santa Suit), no costume could hide his deranged passion even if he were not already an escaped convict. This time Shaw comes as a ghost, anonymously tilting the world from an ironic underground bunker, Castle, and, if possible, he has sunk even deeper into the dark waters of evil.

In yet another display of supreme knowledge, he manages to "implicate Chuck in a massive conspiracy and capture his girl, all from an 8 x 8 cell." The plan began soon after his arrest during his interrogation by Clyde Decker. The Ring Intersect flashed, and in a moment "knew all his dirty secrets." For the next two years Shaw concocted a strategy, spending "every waking second" in his cell "perfecting it." Blackmailing Decker was "easy", and soon he had elements of the CIA working for him. Thus, after engineering the retrieval and release of the Omen virus to open his prison cell door, he moves quickly to nab an unsuspecting Sarah in Castle, string her up like a rack of lamb by the wrists, and lock down the base, giving him both the protection and leverage needed to send Chuck to retrieve the Macau Device from Decker's office. Knowing "the resulting data influx could fry [the mainframe] in seconds" once the 'virus' is released, Shaw, wearing a parka, also takes the precaution of lowering the temperature of Castle to frosty levels. Ultimately, though, he plans not to unleash the virus world-wide but, in conjunction with the Macau Device, relocate all government data into his brain before wiping its computers clean, effectively creating the Intersect 3.0 and making himself so indispensable that the CIA will "have to make him a spy again." One more detail: to deceive Chuck, he even craftily manipulates Sarah to record her voice and, using a computer, enables himself to speak as Sarah.

The same old Shaw gloats over his seeming omnipotence as well. With his scheme appearing to progress well, he turns to Sarah to declare, "You know what the best part is? There's nothing that Chuck can do to stop me." Later, he varies his boastful mockery in Sarah's own voice using the hand-held device, claiming, "This is Sarah Walker, and Daniel Shaw is in complete control of me."

Shaw's tweaked sexuality flashes, too, though it's partly masked by the need to obtain samples of Sarah's voice. In lurid fashion, her former lover and would-be assassin croons, "I've missed you...What we had was special. I know you felt it. I'm sure you've laid in bed at night thinking about me beside you." Once he has the voice samples he requires, Shaw still proceeds to fantasize in Sarah's voice: "Shaw's so handsome and smart." Later, Shaw grabs the half-conscious Sarah roughly by the hair and kisses her. When she comes to, calling him "a sick son of a bitch," he replies that he is just seeing "if any of the old fire was still there" before taking Sarah's charm bracelet as "a token of our last night together."

Shaw can't be any clearer about his motive this time around either. When Chuck first asks him on the phone, his former boss remains a bit cagey: "Because you put me in jail? Because of our last fight? Because you tried to kill me? So much history, Chuck. It could be anything." But with Sarah, Shaw proves more explicit: "This really is about you. See, I'm finally going to crush your soul the way that you crushed mine." And when Sarah, half-frozen to death, attempts to correct Shaw's persistent delusion, citing points he himself made in the initial arc while maintaining his sheep's disguise, it only causes Shaw to delve deeper into his icy heart:

> **Sarah**: I had no idea she was your wife, Shaw. I had no idea who you were. I was just on an assignment.
>
> **Shaw**: Mm. Is that supposed to make me feel better?
>
> **Sarah**: I was just a young agent. I was doing my job, okay? You, of all people, need to understand that.
>
> **Shaw**: Really? Well, what about the pit you dug out of my chest? Is that supposed to fill it in?
>
> **Sarah**: Is this going to? You're a good man, Shaw. You can be that man again. Just stop what you're doing, please…. You can let this all go.

Thus, just as Chuck did on the bridge over the Seine, Sarah makes a last appeal to any shred of virtue that may linger within Shaw. Alas, the result is the same as in Paris: "I know you're in pain, and you want this to stop, but not yet. Not until you feel a pain more excruciating than you ever imagined," a pain that will include watching him kill Chuck while she watches on the Castle screen.

Just as Chuck outwits Shaw in "vs. Ring Part II", the seemingly omniscient one "seriously underestimate[s] the power of the Nerd Herd" in "vs. Santa Suit" as well. Turning out to be a "much bigger nerd than you thought I was," Chuck perceives Shaw's plan, with the help of Jeffster and Shaw himself. Hearing 'Sarah' call him "Dear" on the phone, Chuck realizes both that Shaw has manipulated her and, consequently, is not indeed under lockdown in Castle. Also, when Jeffster concludes the virus is targeting only government computers, it enables Chuck to figure out Shaw's real designs: to relocate the CIA data into his brain, become the Intersect 3.0, and wipe the computers clean. With this information, Chuck is able to modify the Macau Device before Shaw uses it. Consequently, Shaw downloads the Omen virus, deleting the Intersect 2.0 from his brain and rendering him unable to flash. Chuck is equally shrewd when Shaw shows up in the Buy More with the gun, encouraging Shaw's desire to "enjoy" his killing of Chuck in a hand-to-hand combat Shaw is certain he will win rather than simply blowing his unarmed adversary away. When Chuck gains the advantage in that duel, Shaw, with no detonator to reach for this time, cravenly goes for his gun...until Ellie Bartowski plays the part of Sarah and knocks him cold.

In retrospect, the imagery permeating "vs. Santa Suit" figuratively reinforces Shaw's tragic, unanchored moral shift displayed on the plot level of the episode. The text draws attention to this dynamic through a pair of obscure puns pointedly inserted into Shaw's discussion of the retrieval of the Macau Device with Chuck over the phone. Before telling Chuck to "*figure* it out," Shaw checks to see if Chuck is following the instructions by asking, "Get my *drift?*" Accordingly, the Omen virus metaphorically images the destructive influence of Shaw's malice, which succeeds in frying the mainframe of his mind and threatens to destroy others as well.

But there's more in the details. Since the Macau Device facilitates the relocation and wiping out of data on the government computers, it implies the role of either his wife's death or his persistent malice in effecting Shaw's complete moral transfer from virtue to evil. And given that the ownership of Macau, a former colony, had recently been transferred to the sovereign rule of another nation, the otherwise odd name ascribed to the device accents this moral transfer. Also, the icy hell that Shaw creates to prevent the potential overheating of the mainframe, notably achieved after tapping in to Castle's "internal generator", figures the declining moral state of his own making and in which he remains frozen, leading him sadistically to abuse Sarah as she slips into hypothermia and desire Chuck's death as well.

What's in a name? When it comes to CIA Special Agent Daniel Shaw, perhaps more than meets the eye in one last respect. Besides the dual meanings associated with his surname, discussed above, "Windsor Night", the name of the mission on which Chuck flashes during his flight to Paris in the initial arc—soon after Shaw's metaphysical "birthday"—proves one more apt example. In the end, the once God-like agent, suggested by the reference to Windsor, the family surname of English monarchy ruling by Divine Right, becomes increasingly enveloped in the night of evil, a darkness from which he never emerges. Even after his third foiling, Shaw's unrepentant response is only to harm Sarah in any way he still can, namely threatening the life of the child she risked her life to save five years before. The final words with which the Windsor Night leaves viewers prove as pathetic as his bruised and bloodied face through the prison window, his malice evidencing one last death throw: "One thing's going to keep me warm at night. Little something I put into motion that you'll never be able to stop. Does Chuck know about the baby?" Thankfully, Team Bartowski ensures that even Shaw's final scheme will not succeed (See Chapter 14: Sarah vs. Baby).

Chapter 13: Volkoff

The Grand Illusion

With palate poised in one hand and paint brush in the other, the middle-aged executive touches up the canvas tucked along the side of his spacious high rise office, snowflakes silently floating to earth beyond the window behind him. Stepping back without taking beaming eyes off the creation, the self-confessed "hopeless romantic" smiles with pride at his handiwork (vs. Gobbler). Viewers expecting to behold an impressionistic landscape or country picnic party gracing the canvas may find their brows furrowed when instead staring at the portrait of a beagle, which just happens to imitate the statue of a hunting dog guarding the desk nearby.

Welcome to the skewed romantic vision of global arms dealer Alexei Volkoff. Though the dog is proverbially considered man's loyal best friend, that dynamic is decidedly twisted for those employed at Volkoff Industries, where the CEO demands slavish obedience—and success— at the risk of one's life. As the self-styled Russian himself admits to Frost, "You know I get great pleasure from bending people to my will" (vs. Gobbler). Just ask his "top dog" Yuri, better known as The Gobbler (unfortunately, he eats victims). To "earn…an unparalleled place" in Volkoff's organization it "cost him an eyeball" as the carrier of the precious Hydra network. However, his master does not return such sacrificial loyalty. Despite waxing on about his "love to work with this man" and their "long and storied history," disappointment over lack of access to his Hydra network while Yuri sat in prison quickly leaves the former head canine a corpse for the clean-up crew. Similarly, when another lieutenant doesn't meet Volkoff's standard, his boss nonchalantly informs Frost, "I had to let him go…off a 20-story building" (vs. Push Mix). Ironically, such brutality endears the 'rogue' Sarah to him. Volkoff applauds both Sarah's claim to allegedly "use" Casey in proving her newfound loyalty to him because "he's still loyal to me" and her launching of him to his supposed death out a Los Angeles high-rise window (vs. Gobbler).

Of course, Alexei is the real top dog of Volkoff Industries, rendering his painting a Narcissistic and bizarre self-portrait. However, the Moscow-based Hunting Hound pursues a much grander vision than simply serving as master to a pack of lapdogs. Betraying his aspiration to become the "world's biggest bad-ass, killer of men, conqueror of nations" (vs. Family Volkoff), the megalomaniac plans to unleash his plan of global domination through the recovered Hydra network hidden in the eyeball he unflinchingly scoops out of dead Yuri's socket. Pointedly called "the heart of Volkoff Industries" and "more important than Volkoff himself" (vs. Gobbler), the "infrastructure" allows him to communicate with his sundry minions, who he purposely prevents from knowing each other. With more than a tad of hubris, Volkoff, accordingly, claims that the Hydra eyeball enables him to "see everything." Alas, the fact that the eyeball, notably a fake, is utterly crushed by his own hand (with the hound statue no less) implies the irony of his claim. Indeed, his many-headed vision of both others and himself, highlighted by the mythological source of its name, will ultimately reveal itself as nothing but a grand illusion due to the "flaw" of his own "human error."

In one false vision, the Moscow-based arms dealer exhibits a decidedly dim view of Frost, a dynamic pointedly imaged during a cell phone conversation they share in "vs. Push Mix". While Sarah notably accesses the Hydra network, Frost purposely takes the Skype call in a shadowy corner of Volkoff's office, making visibility difficult and leading Volkoff to comment, "It's really dark there." In contrast, he proves clearly visible on the screen of Frost, who emphasizes the point: "I can see you." Likewise, Volkoff cannot see past Frost's outward loyalty to him, convinced he has turned her as a double agent, while she precisely envisions him as a "the world's biggest psychopath" (vs. Leftovers). When Frost voices her faux concern over his accepting the allegedly traitorous Sarah into his organization, Volkoff mistakenly points to Frost's own experience as proof she need not worry: "Remember your intentions when you first met me? Now you're my right hand" (vs. Gobbler). Later, he confidently expresses similar sentiments to Chuck when Sarah, assigned to 'kill'

Casey, is poised to take a "leap" of loyalty, claiming, "Your mother made it all those years ago."

Volkoff proves equally blind when envisioning himself as a legitimate candidate for the love of Frost, with whom he is utterly obsessed. Confusing her seeming professional commitment to him with a latent desire for him, even though they have "never been together," he claims "he had no choice" but to bring a team to Burbank and incinerate the CIA base below if Frost is not released (vs. Leftovers). And when he reneges on his promise to let the Castle Crew live after Frost is released, he justifies the lie: "In my defense, you threatened the woman I love." Still, the megalomaniac's delusion resurfaces when stating, in case she is not released, that he "rather she die than live without me," and he further misguidedly asserts that Frost will embrace his execution of Chuck as a "romantic gesture." In the end, the shattering of the bizarre illusion focused upon his "sweet little pea" leaves him an utterly pathetic figure (vs. Push Mix).

When Frost shrewdly claims that Chuck uses her love against her to save them both at the Buy More, it elicits a sympathetic response from her wannabe lover: "We always expect the best from the ones we love… and rarely get it" (vs. Leftovers). Of course, he speaks with dramatic irony given that his love, Frost, will ultimately 'betray' him. Before she does, though, Frost first tries to bring a smidgen of clarity to his world, exposing Volkoff as not a hopeless romantic but a slavish master when asserting, "You don't know how to love someone; you only know how to control them" (vs. Leftovers). Of course, discovering her real identity as a double agent on the Countessa crushes his false vision and leaves him pining, "I believed in you" (vs. Push Mix). And when the last fragments are swept away by Mary Bartowski's claim to have been thinking about Stephen every hour she was with Volkoff, he proves so devastated that he fully intends to let her die along with his fantasy.

Frost isn't the only double agent that pulls the wool over Volkoff's eyes. Sarah's ruse of disarming the C.E.O.'s guards and then leaving Volkoff unharmed makes him a believer in her alibi of "cashing out [to] buy a future with the man I love," though the narrative is ironically true (vs. Gobbler). And when putting her to the ultimate test, killing Casey, the Castle spies' devious, impromptu scheme of selecting a window with a hanging platform a few stories beneath goes undetected (though Casey still almost loses his life) to the point that Volkoff urges Chuck to give

Sarah space, explaining, "Taking a leap like this is painful for all involved. But congratulations: you're one step closer to the woman you love." In a final irony, Volkoff, his eyes wide shut, still tries to open Chuck's: "Don't you *see*, Charles? She did this for you."

Chuck and his father take their turns exposing Volkoff's myopia, too. Confident of Frost's professional loyalty, and hopeful it will extend to the romantic realm, the Stalin-era holdover actually voices his own ignorance when stating, "It's really pathetic. Orion spent his whole life searching for a woman that didn't want to be found." And Volkoff doubles the irony by projecting his own delusion on to his rival: "[Orion] meant nothing to her...the [woman] he so much wanted to believe in" (vs. First Fight). In another twist, Volkoff's jealousy leads him to deem Chuck's faux messages to Frost from Orion authentic, and he goes to prison raging, "You've been talking to Orion every day for years, night after night, behind my back!" (vs. Push Mix).

Volkoff proves blind to Chuck's qualities as well. Only after Frost holds his finger on the trigger, saving Chuck at the Buy More, does the realization hit that he is her son ("So this is why he isn't dead"), and he proceeds to "underestimate" Chuck on not one but two occasions (vs. Leftovers). After escaping from Orion's base before it is blown up, Chuck regroups to trick the man who likes to quote Stalin into speaking the Hydra password phrase ("Death is the solution to all problems") and holding him at bay with a pistol containing no bullets (vs. Push Mix). Just prior, Volkoff, still convinced of his invulnerability, tells Chuck that he cannot put a bullet between the eyes of his self-styled stepfather because Volkoff, like the Hydra network, has "access to everyone," including the people Chuck loves, and adds he will "need an army" to leave Orion's cabin alive. Of course, Chuck anticipates Volkoff's moves and leaves his vanquished foe with a ironic lesson he gleaned from his father: "Looks can be deceiving."

However, no false vision—not even that involving Frost—proves as painful when exposed as that concerning his daughter. Vivian cannot grasp how someone she "barely knew" could be "watching me this whole time," a realization that comes from receiving the necklace key and reviewing the photos and clippings from the safe deposit box recovered from the bank in Macau (vs. Bank of Evil). Indeed, Volkoff deemed her his "succession plan" (vs. Masquerade), his "chosen successor" groomed from her youth. As Boris, her failed assassin details, "You were skeet shooting at age seven, had your black belt at 13 and by the time you graduated from the London School of Economics, you were fluent in five languages." And though she initially resists the temptation, she appears poised to make Volkoff's vision a reality when he receives evidence of her evil baptism, imaged by the watermark he observes on the Volkoff stationary when holding it up to the prison light.

As he leads the Castle Crew to the Swiss military bunker holding the thorium, and thus a functional Norseman weapon, Volkoff sees himself on the cusp of attaining his grandiose spectacle. All that remains is to betray Chuck and formalize the alliance with Vivian. However, when she arrives, Vivian does the "twisting". The father who thinks his daughter will yearn to hear his introductory letter read in his self-styled Russian accent (by Reilly, comically) also misreads her actions at the climactic moment (vs. Bank of Evil). Once she gets her hands on the thorium (vs. Family Volkoff), she rejects his vision of co-ruling "partners" along with the necklace and photos, "tokens from a stranger," with crystal clarity: "I don't know you! I will never know you!" Ironically, Vivian tells her father he succeeded as her schoolmaster all too well: "Trust no one! You taught me that!" she claims, leaving Volkoff to moan, "That didn't include me." In the shattering aftermath, his bluster vanishing as fast as his familial vision of world domination, he realizes, "She hates me...Just let me die...I failed her."

Though the prospect of a future without Vivian cuts more deeply than the exposure of any of his other false visions, Volkoff's confrontation with his real identity is, at least initially, just as tragic. From his arrest at Orion's cabin up to the extraction of the flawed Intersect prototype from his brain, Volkoff evidences a "spiritual growth...constantly evolving" towards a clearer picture of his evil self and his harming of others, a dynamic figured by the Darwinian-inspired chess game he plays to enter the Swiss bunker (vs. Family Volkoff). However, it is an intense struggle punctuated by defeats before victory is claimed.

It begins in his sessions with Dr. Nelson, his 'avatar' at River Hill Penitentiary (implied by the movie Volkoff claims to watch in prison the week prior), who enlightens Volkoff on his "entitlement issues," even if now limited to cutting the cafeteria line (vs. Family Volkoff). As he informs Chuck and Sarah during their visit to retrieve him for a mission, "A major part of recovery is seeing the opposing points of view," and he claims to desire "making apologies to all the people I've harmed, making amends," particularly with Vivian and Frost. But just as he points out to pirate Ellyas Abshir in Mogadishu, Volkoff's "morality is in a state of development" and remains a "work in progress." Indeed, from the moment Chuck and Sarah enter the penitentiary to the moment before Vivian exposes his illusion of a family dynasty, the erstwhile poster child of criminal reform proves more than ready to put his spiritual evolution on the back burner, "have some fun," and resurrect his vision of global domination. As he himself admits, "Old thinking: it creeps back in."

However, Vivian's betrayal, which holds his life up to the mirror of her hatred, impacts Volkoff so deeply that it leads to permanent change. Not coincidentally, he activates the portable EMP he smuggles into the cave, pointedly "this year's innovation," to keep Vivian from killing them all and enabling him to begin pursuing an innovated life (vs. Family Volkoff). No doubts on this matter remain when, before being rolled back to River Hill in chains, he confesses to Frost, "I've done terrible things. I've been evil….Money, greed and power are a dance with Satan. And he looks like me." Likewise, he achieves clarity of vision regarding his relationship with Frost, telling her, "I was drawn to the goodness in you…I was not worthy of your love like Orion was. Please accept my apology and know that I'm trying to improve."

No sooner does Volkoff come to grips with his real nature than fate confronts him with another shocker: the revelation of his real identity as Hartley Winterbottom, an English scientist "gentle as a lamb" who didn't like guns (vs. Cliffhanger). Of course the news comes compliments of Clyde Decker, who suppresses the flawed program in his mind moments before Chuck arrives on the Night Hawk to whisk him away to save Sarah, and it leaves Hartley without any memory of his past as Volkoff. Hartley's amazement over his "fictitious profile" is pointedly imaged when he stands in Casey's apartment incredulously staring at his face in a mirror. And when further informed of the evil "monster" of a person he was (again recalling his many-headed Hydra vision), as well as the particularly devastating impact of his life on his daughter, Hartley is left to call himself "a bloody fool" for insisting that his "old friend," Stephen Bartowski, "use his computer program to help me."

The good news, though, is that Hartley receives the opportunity to pursue a new and improved vision before the curtain falls. Barely. Hartley enlists in the attempt to save Sarah's life by mixing up a batch of antidote, Iridium 5, only to find it an older generation concoction that merely extends Sarah's life by hours (vs. Last Details). But when he arrives at Volkoff Industries with Chuck to find the Iridium 6 it is believed he made in secret during his years as Volkoff, he suddenly balks at going through with the plan. Overwhelmed by the reality of meeting a daughter he grievously harmed and does not remember, he explains, "W-What do you say to a daughter you've never even met? 'I'm sorry I've ruined your life?' No. No." But managing to marshal those fears, he reappears in time not only to save Chuck and Sarah's lives but also administer the antidote for Vivian's anger and fear. After confirming that Chuck never betrayed her and the 'fault' of becoming Volkoff was really his own, Hartley proceeds to offer her alternative visions of herself and a salvaged family (with the pointed help of some clean identities): "Vivian, I don't know you, but I'd like to. If you pull that trigger, you'll lose yourself like I did." With a bit of coaxing, she accepts the promise of both.

Before turning the page on Volkoff, it is worthwhile to consider a similar metaphor that works in concert with the Hydra eyeball. Within the context of Volkoff's many-headed grand illusion, the game of charades played at the Bartowski Thanksgiving leftovers evening takes on added significance (vs. Leftovers). Granted, the role-playing entertainment certainly links to the specific false roles Volkoff assumes for the evening, including Frost's friendly MI6 handler and her children's kindly pseudo-stepfather. However, the charade ultimately links with Volkoff's overarching false vision of himself, a point that becomes even more intriguing when one recalls the movie twice guessed incorrectly: "The Bourne Identity". Robert Ludlum's espionage classic presents another amnesiac spy who spends much of the story searching for information about his real identity before finally reassuming it in the end. As long as Volkoff remained blind to his actual identity, and did not seek it, he could not imitate Jason Bourne. With his grand illusion as Volkoff destroyed and his real sense of self restored, would Hartley instead choose to mimic the Ludlum hero during a future round of the game? Actually, it's a trick question: he doesn't play charades anymore.

Chapter 14: "Chuck vs. The Baby"

Sarah vs. The Baby

Most every one of "Chuck's" 91 episodes reaches a standard of quality making it worthy of the viewer's time. However, several episodes prove themselves crafted with a verbal and visual sophistication that sets them in a separate category of cinematographic literature. Some come in trios, like the Introductory and Jill arcs, while others come in closely linked pairs, including "vs. Fear of Death"/"Phase Three" and "vs. Sarah"/"Goodbye". In addition to these, a few stand-alone episodes stand apart, "vs. Santa Claus" and "vs. Ring" among them (For analyses devoted to each of these examples, see *Unpacking "Chuck"* and Chapter 5 of this volume). To this latter group belongs the series' last masterfully produced individual episode: "Chuck vs. The Baby". A gripping chronicle of Mollie's rescue from Ryker in its own right, "vs. Baby" also evidences a complex intertwining of script and imagery to complete the series-long saga of Sarah's emotional salvation as it plays out in strikingly parallel fashion.

The episode opens with a flashback to a stormy Hungarian night, the evening on which Sarah's former CIA handler turned to the dark side. Quarterbacking a mission four to five years in the past, Ryker, whose surname is pointedly derived from a German word for "rich", sits inside a car parked outside a Budapest mansion while ordering Sarah to enter, kill the eleven thugs that have slaughtered the owners, and bring out the "package", a baby girl she finds in a crib. Throughout the sequence, the windows of Ryker's vehicle, drenched with streaking raindrops, imply his nefarious baptism. As Ryker himself admits to Sarah the next day, "[The baby's] the only heir to a massive fortune, so whoever has her has access to it. She's the key." Sensing the "rotten" nature of his rogue mission, Sarah exposes Ryker's assertion of altruism in killing the parents' murderers as well as the pretext that he is owed something to compensate for living a secret life beyond the grasp of loved ones, noting, "…You don't have a family. That money is just for you."

But getting his hands on the package isn't simply a case of white collar crime. Agent Walker has the intuition to further inquire about what's going to happen to the baby when Ryker takes the money. Citing the girl's legitimate claim to the fortune, she presses the matter to its head: "You expect me to believe that you're going to let her live?" The only answer her handler provides at the time is an obstruction: "That's above your pay grade." However, years later, when events reach their climax in Emma's kitchen, he reveals the real answer: "I'm gonna kill you and then I'm gonna kill your mom. And then after I get that money, you know what I'm gonna do with that little girl?" Accordingly, Ryker's arrival to that very scene reprises his transfer to the realm of moral darkness when his disembodied shadow, preceding him, passes through brilliant sunlight until consumed by the shade while crossing Emma's front lawn.

Ryker's corruption frames the balance of the episode. Each of the flashback scenes set in Hungary, including the opening sequence, are pointedly filmed with a dark filter, implying not merely the dangerous shadow world Sarah inhabits but, given selective images of muted light, also the moral dichotomy of good and evil with which Sarah is now faced: either aiding and abetting the theft and ultimate murder of the child to appease her superior or defy him to save its fragile life at the risk of her own. Upon Sarah's entry into the dimly lit mansion, the lens initially links the Agent of Light to the glowing chandeliers, below which she pauses, before she proceeds to flip, cartwheel, shoot, and knife her way through the grand dining room in fantastic fashion. But Agent Walker finds herself thrown for another loop by what she finds waiting for her in a bedroom: a baby, dressed all in white, bathed in the room's only pool of dull light, a visual effect repeated in the scenes set in her Budapest hotel room. Ultimately, Ryker's treachery forces Sarah to make a decision as tumultuous as the discordant Budapest night on which she finds the baby. Indeed, the precipitation, thunder and lightning permeating the mansion and hotel room scenes echo the dynamics surrounding another traumatic decision she will make two to three years in her future to safeguard the possibility of a future with Chuck (See *Unpacking "Chuck"* Chapter 7: Thunder and Rain).

When Sarah chooses light over darkness, her virtuous decision, in turn, initiates her own rogue mission as the child's self-appointed guardian angel. The lullaby scene foregrounds this role, as Sarah, clearly out of her element with the crying baby, seeks the help of her marginalized mother on the phone. Emma advises her daughter that the baby needs to feel safe and warm, a point Sarah herself later reinforces by telling her mother that the child likes to be wrapped in a blanket. After that alone does not succeed in soothing the baby, Emma suggests singing a familiar childhood lullaby, with significant success:

> Slumber, my darling
> Your mother is near
> Guarding your dreams
> From all terror and fear
> Sunlight has past
> And the twilight has gone
> Slumber, my darling
> And the night's coming on.

Accordingly, Sarah, the blissfully ignorant baby's pseudo-mother, proceeds to risk not only life and limb but also the potentially precious relationship with her own mother to protect the child and its future from the approaching nightmare cast by Ryker's moral darkness.

Sarah's first act of radical rebellion consists of wounding Ryker before he unloads on her from beneath the café tablecloth, and subsequently running for their lives, even if the baby never left the safety of the hotel room. Within that shadowy room, with the baby again bathed in dull light, Sarah seeks the Stateside guarantee of the child's protection from a sympathetic Director Graham before she confirms her possession of "the package", a guarantee he simply cannot provide. Noting the paperwork the CIA would require in taking possession of the child, Graham acknowledges there will be "records that a man like Ryker might be able to get his hands on." With the rainwater streaking across the hotel room window pointedly shadowing her face, ironically recalling the drenched windows of Ryker's car and his turn to the dark side, Sarah's emotional reconfiguration continues by informing Graham, "I'm not in possession of the package, Director" (For more on the early stages of Sarah's internal transformation see *Unpacking "Chuck"* Chapter 2: Fish Out of Water).

When leaving the baby with the mother no one knows exists, Sarah confirms the exorbitant cost she will assume for her virtue: "For both of you to be safe, I can never see you again." Before she leaves, though, the baby's protector desires to secure more than just the baby's life but also its long-term well-being. With final wishes that betray the price she has already paid for pursuing her shadow life, Sarah pleads, "Um, going to prom and, um, soccer games and…and all those normal things that you wanted for me: will you just make sure that she gets them?"

To guarantee this promise of a normal life, Sarah leaves an emergency device disguised as a shiny, ring-shaped rattle; when activated, it receives a signal: the coordinates for locating a safe house if The Nightmare ever returns. Alas, he does, but warned and guided by the signal, Emma ushers Mollie to safety before Ryker strolls across the front lawn to pointedly kick the soccer ball aside even as he intends to thrust aside the normal life Mollie has been given. Moreover, Ryker remains ignorant of the fact that Mollie's guardian angel has already descended upon the house with a righteous anger to judge him. The victor of a violent confrontation with the evil Sand Man, Sarah forcefully preserves both Mollie's present and future by skewering Ryker through the stomach with a carving knife, blood smeared across her face. And even as her wide-eyed former handler settles to his knees, the last words he hears voice the fulfillment of Sarah's holy purpose: "She'll never have nightmares, and she'll never even know that you existed. She's going to have the life that she deserves, a normal one."

Though Mollie's rescue and Sarah's conquest over a moral dilemma prove compelling drama, these plot lines share the stage with another significant narrative that ironically reprises some of the episode's imagery: the final stage of Sarah's years-long emotional surrender to Chuck. By Season 5, Sarah has walked a long path to reach the point of marriage and the anticipation of starting a family with a profession that matches (see *Unpacking "Chuck"* Chapter 16: All Roads Lead to Home). Indeed, by "vs. Baby" viewers no longer recognize the Agent Walker whose "file screamed loner" and "never trusted anyone". Still, when Sarah receives word that Shaw has informed Ryker of the baby's existence, it touches a nerve from the past embedded so deeply that it exposes a lingering emotional response perhaps as shocking to Sarah as to Chuck.

The electrifying news comes to her husband, ironically, during a candle-lit preview of the Dream House. No sooner has Chuck enthusiastically imagined the interior décor of their potential home than he observes the troubled exterior of Sarah's countenance. And when pursuing the source of the matter he soon comes to realize it's not a "negotiable" issue as simple as where to locate the game chairs. Informed, "Something urgent has come up," Chuck, typically happy to come alongside, asks, "What is it? You know you can tell me anything." But his wife offers only an enigma in reply: "Well, that's just it. This time, Chuck, I can't tell you."

Enter the baggage motif. The next scene in Castle opens with the foregrounding of Sarah checking a pistol chamber to ensure it is loaded, even as Chuck reminds Sarah of her own words voiced a season before: "No more secrets." On the heels of this image, Sarah pointedly folds the legs of a high-powered gun and loads it in her bag before zipping it shut, hoisting the heavy burden over her shoulder and preparing to leave for Budapest, alone. Accordingly, Sarah's mouth remains zipped about exactly what's weighing her down. However, when Chuck intervenes as the CEO of Carmichael Industries who asks no questions and offers the company's pro bono aid, Sarah waivers: "It wouldn't change anything. There are still things I can't tell you." After the condition is met and she accepts the offer, Sarah pointedly drops the bag to the floor with a thud, though it remains full. Thus, when even tight-lipped Casey attempts to know her secret, Sarah still declines, though tenderly using his first name: "I appreciate that, John. But the less you know, the better. Really."

Consequently, when the team reaches Budapest, Chuck and Casey's view into Sarah's inner turmoil initially remains detached. The binoculars and scope they use, respectively, to observe her meet with Ryker at the cafe across the street from the hotel room figure this dynamic (while also foreshadowing the imminent insight they will gain into Sarah's plight). Similarly, when called down to the street to track the waiter who delivered Ryker's message, their only view of a still-conflicted Sarah is a receding one through the rear window of a bus as she mouths to Chuck, "I've got to go do this alone." Of course, Sarah soon sees the folly of her solitary mission when her decision leaves her bound to a chair at Ryker's mercy. However, Ryker's mockery adds insult to the sting of her facial blows, implying that Sarah's current bondage is ultimately the result of her remaining emotional baggage: "I knew [5 years ago] that you could keep a secret, because you had no one to tell. And you still don't, do you? I bet no one even knows that you're here, do they? And that's why you're gonna die today...."

Within this context, the episode's guardian imagery takes an ironic twist, with Chuck reprising the protector role Sarah plays with Mollie even as Sarah assumes the role of the one (heart-)warmed and protected. A pair of key scenes play out this intriguing figurative shift. Initially, Chuck, along with Casey, finds his way to Sarah by breaking Ryker's messenger and promptly overcoming Ryker's defenses. Pointedly calling Sarah "Baby", Chuck quickly unties her bonds and they escape, foreshadowing his role in her final liberation from the fears that restrain her from fully trusting him in deeds and not just words.

This scene is followed by perhaps the most crucial of the episode, and one in which Chuck again addresses her as "Babe". Home from Hungary, Chuck watches over Sarah, who slumbers like a child beneath a warm blanket, as she drifts "in and out" of sleep, likely implying her emotional ambivalence. Meanwhile, Chuck also takes it upon himself to unpack her bags and put her clothes away in the closet, which otherwise improbably features a pair of girl's roller skates sitting on the top shelf. By no coincidence, Chuck proceeds to help Sarah begin to unpack her internal turmoil when she awakens not only literally but, metaphorically, to the folly of her residual emotional independence as well. Ironically, this moment was also foreshadowed by none other than Ryker years before at their Budapest café meet. "Listen," he predicted, "I know this job is the only thing in your life, but someday you're gonna realize it's not enough, that keeping your whole life a secret from everyone who loves you is too much."

In the end, Sarah proves Ryker a prophet. In self-admittedly uncharacteristic fashion, Chuck, deeply troubled by Sarah's decision to "hide…the truth" and go "out on [her] own", assumes the risk of gently confronting Sarah, not only calling it "a mistake" but quietly insisting, "…You were wrong." To his relief, his bride concurs. After confessing that she trusts him "completely" and wants to tell him "everything", Sarah finally provides a front row view into her turmoil by recalling her thoughts while bound in Budapest: "I kept thinking 'Why am I doing it this way?' Why do I have to do everything on my own. It's what my dad taught me. It's the way the CIA taught me: that you can ever only trust yourself." Equally significant, Sarah voices recognition of the revolution within herself. In the episode's final scene, set again at the Dream House they now won't be able to afford, Sarah affirms, "I'm different now. Things have changed. You've changed me." And just as he does earlier

136

in their bedroom after Sarah awakes, Chuck again takes his heart-warmed babe into his arms and holds her close.

Sarah subsequently matches her words with deeds. Acting on her internal revolution, she tells Chuck the full story about her mother and the baby. And when The Nightmare comes calling, Sarah doesn't hesitate to bring Chuck and Casey with her. A good thing, too. Knowing his several henchmen wait outside, Ryker taunts the seemingly solitary Sarah when he briefly gains the upper hand in their struggle: "But you always manage to make the same mistake. Even when you have a team, here you are all alone. When the hell are you gonna learn?" But when gun shots and fisticuffs erupt outside, startling Ryker with the proof of her transformation, Sarah delivers the triumphant punch line: "I didn't come alone."

The vicious duel between Sarah and Ryker proves saturated with imagery figuring this profound change. When Ryker enters the kitchen, water pointedly pours from the faucet before Sarah turns it off, suddenly pulls her submerged pistol out of the filled sink, and turns to face her enemy with her arm extended and the weapon still dripping. From there, visions of her shattered emotional boundaries come in quick succession: Sarah's head crashes through the glass of a cabinet door moments before a wine bottle disintegrates over her head (For similar imagery pertaining to Chuck, see *Unpacking "Chuck"* Chapter 14: Phase III). Before the battle is over, Sarah even punches through a wall into Mollie's room! And after finally subduing Ryker, Sarah rushes outside to view the already evident blessing of her inner reconfiguration: Chuck & Casey finishing off the henchmen that surely would have overwhelmed her had she come alone.

In the final analysis, the signal device that Sarah leaves with Emma serves a key metaphorical function, too. In one regard, their mutual encounter with Mollie ends up helping Sarah permanently find her way home to Emma, whose anguished phone call leads off the episode: "I want you to know, if you ever feel like you need a place to come home to, well, you have one." The deep, prolonged embrace they share in the closing scene is accented with the simple but heart-felt words the former "tough little thing" manages to whisper: "I missed you."

However, the overarching emphasis of the signal imagery points towards the completion of Sarah's process in finding her emotional residence with Chuck. A year prior, Sarah confessed to Chuck, "You're my home. Always have been" (vs. Suitcase). This point is driven home when Emma, waiting for Sarah's arrival at the apartment, notably marvels at the photos chronicling Mr. and Mrs. Bartowski's intimate, shared life, ironizing the daughter who "always kept to herself...[and] wouldn't let people get close." Overwhelmed with gratitude, Emma feels compelled to tell Chuck, "I know I don't know you really well yet, but thank you for giving her this." Still incredulous some minutes later, Emma asks Sarah, "Ever think [your CIA career] would *lead* you here?" Mrs. Bartowski's answer is poignant: "No, but, ah, Chuck has taught me that every now and then it's OK to be surprised."

But when Mollie's rattle pointedly settles on the Bartowski's coffee table at the episode's conclusion, the metaphor extends to imply Chuck as Sarah's personal safe house. She locates this secure destination by virtue of finally trusting her husband with her most deeply held secret when, recalling Mollie's plight, the nightmare of her past returns to haunt her present. Indeed, when Sarah pleads in the van while racing to Emma's house, "I sent her the coordinates. I just hope she remembers the signal....Please remember the signal, please," she actually projects her own struggle to achieve full and permanent intimacy. Ultimately, Sarah remembers the coordinates of her personal Intersect—namely his utter trustworthiness and unyielding love—and meets him in his heart-warming arms.

Chapter 15: Jeffster

The Flames of Destiny

"Is it really your destiny to be a complete moron?" Though Big Mike directs these words specifically to Lester as late as "vs. Bullet Train", they could apply just as easily to Jeff or to them as a pair through the majority of the series. On all three counts, though, Big Mike's question ultimately turns out to be an ironic one. Not only do both Jeff and Lester succeed in completing their individual treks (see Chapters 4 & 8), but their paths also converge in a shared journey, leading them to a destination few could have imagined.

Jeff and Lester, as implied by "Jeffster", the name chosen for the musical band they form, prove inseparable partners in a variety of ways, including some so pathetically dysfunctional that the duo often becomes a comic caricature. When dressing up for Halloween (vs. Sand Worm), they coordinate their costumes, reprising Grant Wood's iconic painting "American Gothic", which presents a haggard, pitchfork-holding farmer and his wife. Of course, the choice is an ironic one, given that hard labor is the last thing on either one's mind, especially when in the company of the other. In fact, if there is any crop the two cultivate while at the Buy More, it's idleness. To catalog their work-avoidance artistry in total would require a book of its own, so a selective list must suffice.

Some examples can be placed in the category of the relatively harmless. When not simply telling Buy More customers, even Ellie, that they will not wait on them, whether on break or not (vs. Suitcase), Jeffster engages in thumb wars (vs. Marlin) and organizing the gambling event du jour. In one memorable incident, the pair kidnaps Kevin Bacon (vs. Muurder), the mascot pig of Large Mart, which not only leads to Big Mike's abduction, though that is ameliorated by a Subway foot-long, but ties up Manager

Morgan in mafia-like negotiations for the day to obtain his release. And then the pig goes missing!

In a bit more depraved fashion, Jeffster instigates the Fight Club diversion back in the cage, leaving the Buy More floor empty of personnel, and engages in base thievery in which they stash iPhones on one occasion (vs. Leftovers), and donations from the "shameful" 'Save Jeff Barnes' campaign, complete with wheelchair, on another (vs. Zoom). Jeffster also finds a way to indulge themselves on the Buy More's dime when off the premises. Believing "everyone needs to get their freak on sometimes," they dubiously brag to Casey about going on "installs" twice a week that leave them waking up "in some of the best dumpsters in town" (vs. Couch Lock).

On a more perverted plane, Jeffster also spends hours recording unsuspecting customers—and Pita Palace delivery girls—with the mammary cam (vs. Marlin), that is when not stalking Sarah and even Chuck with a camera (vs. Last Details). In Season 4, Lester boasts to Manager Morgan, "We have over 1,250 hours of Sarah-related footage," before Jeff expounds, "I've had a camera running for years. We have voyeur; we have candids; we have nip slips…of Chuck." The same dynamic reveals itself when Ellie, knowing exactly with whom she is dealing, commits fraud against herself to motivate Jeffster to find the computer Devon allegedly left for repair at the Nerd Herd desk (vs. A-Team). After dismissively instructed to "mush" without a claim slip, she tells them, hesitantly with a bit lip, that the drive has "something… private" on it. When encouraged to elaborate, Ellie alleges that she and Devon "made a video when we were in med school; I'd just hate for it to fall into the wrong hands." Like Pavlovian dogs, they proceed to mush themselves, clearing their schedule to find the laptop "if it's the last thing we do." Is it any wonder, then, that Jeffster's search for 'romance' focuses on the "medium-hot chicks at Underpants Unlimited" (vs. Three Words) and wenches at Renaissance fairs? (vs. First Bank of Evil).

Occasionally, though, Jeffster's time-wasting pranks take on a more rebellious edge, as both Emmett and Morgan know all too well. In response to Emmett's coup d'etat to become the Buy More manager, making idleness more difficult to achieve than under Big Mike's tenure, Jeffster stages its own clandestine revolt. Punning "This will show them who's really in charge," they use a small explosive to blow up the local electrical control panel. Not only do they succeed in their stated goal, shutting down the automated checkout machines, but blacking out the entire block as well, allowing Chuck and Sarah to escape from their Castle lockdown at the hands of Colonel Casey (vs. Colonel). And in the aftermath of Assistant Manager Morgan's putting the kibosh on the Fight Club, Jeffster forms "an evil cabal of tricksters" that teams up to harass Morgan with booby traps, including electrified door handles and glued chairs, as well as spiking coffee with laxatives (vs. First Class). Before Casey resorts to abducting Lester, the ring-leader, for a round of pacifying hypnotism, Jeff, Lester's henchman, is pleased to deliver his buddy's defiant message: "Lester says this isn't over."

However, some of their pranks, whether on or off hours, cause more substantially significant problems. Their impromptu, drunken theft of Big Mike's marlin after hours, a "wasted mission" in more ways than one, complicates a sequence of events that almost results in getting Chuck bunkered in D.C. and delaying Awesome's marriage proposal (vs. Marlin). Worst of all, though, when Lester signs for Chuck's computer from Orion (vs. Lethal Weapon), they subsequently play the new 'video game' in Jeff's office in the Buy More bathroom, only narrowly averting the incineration of two big box stores by a Predator drone without ever knowing the closeness of their own destruction.

Jeffster's propensity for mischief is so pervasive that even when they aren't responsible for a tragedy, they assume they are…with pathetic consequences. Just after Jeff offers Big Mike the favor of burning the Buy More to the ground both to avoid his firing and retaliate for the slated closing of the store (vs. Ring Part II), Jeffster ends up thinking they might have been the culprits in its actual destruction when a broken thumb-swaddled Morgan drops Shaw's detonator. Seeing their mugs on the news as suspects doesn't help. Alas, they spend the next 184 days "runnin' from the po-po," camping out in Jeff's van along the L.A. River a mere seven minutes from Burbank (vs. Suitcase). Bargaining for even basic sustenance, they resort to "exchanging gigs at the Whisper Lounge for strips of tapas." When Casey, along with Morgan, appears from out of the dark to retrieve them, Jeffster determines, in mock heroic fashion, to go down "just like Thelma and Louise" by taking suicide pills. Within moments, though, they shift from suicidal to spoiled, demanding a raise and perks to entice their return to the Buy More, ensuring their tranqing.

As Morgan explains, "They may be idiots, but they're my idiots...Without Jeff and Lester, it would just be another electronics store."

Despite all their buffoonery, Jeff and Lester's partnership occasionally provides glimpses of untapped potential and even impressive capability. They certainly are no slouches with computers in the rare instance they find themselves "incentivized" to work (vs. Santa Suit). In "vs. Tango", Jeffster and Anna spend much of the night in the cage eliminating the significant back log of broken devices, which they likely helped create, in an attempt to avert Harry Tang's ascension to assistant manager. More impressively, the pair, who plead to attend NextExpo at Roark Instruments (vs. Dream Job), "reverse engineer" the Omen Virus in Season 5. Armed with their knowledge of "C++ and a bunch of other computer languages," they determine not only that it is "hypothetically designed to suck information out of a whole set of computers and move that information to a single location," but discover it is targeting only government computers (vs. Santa Suit). Thus, after citing the fact that "no one computer can hold all that information," they logically conclude it is both a hoax and "real-life conspiracy," helping Chuck discern Shaw's plan: to download the data into his brain. Clearly, Jeffster validates Chuck's noteworthy assessment of them: "If they're focused, they're better than any computer expert in the CIA."

With the notable exception of their misguided pursuit of Greta in "vs. Fear of Death", Jeffster demonstrates an equal mastery when it comes to stalking. When Morgan assigns them the task of researching Hannah (vs. First Class), they report the details of her diet, musical tastes, and interest in French cinema in quick time, earning them a follow-up assignment on Chuck. A few episodes later (vs. American Hero), they feel the need to "demonstrate [their] worth" by showing they can "stalk with the best of them" when following Shaw on his sacrificial suicide mission and helping Chuck save the day. After he meets them at The Ring warehouse, Chuck again lavishes them with the highest praise: "You guys are the most amazing stalkers I've ever seen. I'm going to tell my grandchildren about you." And when a desperate Chuck still has doubts about whether they can locate Sarah in the series finale (vs. Goodbye), they laugh at him, replying, "We can find a woman off the discarded remnants of an Outback Bloomin' Onion." Indeed, by "unleash[ing] the perverts," their army of Buy Morons, they succeed in "sniff[ing]...out...

that birdie in flight," ultimately and ironically reporting that Sarah stands at the Nerd Herd desk.

The same dynamic evidences itself in Jeffster's legendary musical pilgrimage, too, though it suffers a rocky start. The duo originally considered calling themselves "Jester", which at the time may have been a more appropriate moniker (vs. Best Friend). Though the first audition to play the Woodcomb's wedding reception never gets off the ground, Jeff succeeds in settling a panicked Lester by affirming, "Partnership is trust," and appealing to Lester to risk it for him if not willing to do it for himself. While the Buy More crowd appears to enjoy the cover of Toto's "Africa", the performance still falls short of earning them the gig. However, they end up providing the pre-wedding entertainment anyway when Ted Roark's appearance calls for a delaying tactic (vs. Ring). Unfortunately, their rendition of Styx's "Mr. Roboto" doesn't impress the groom's father, who asks Devon, "Why are you letting Sam Kinison and an Indian lesbian wreck your wedding?"

In Season 3, the reviews remain far from resounding. While covering Credence Clearwater Revival's "Fortunate Son" during the revolutionary blockade of the Buy More (vs. Beard), the head Ring agent, busy infiltrating Castle, sarcastically comments, "So that's the sound of liberty." Likewise, Big Mike agrees to let Jeffster screen their music video reprising Bon Jovi's "Blaze of Glory", on which they spend two full weekends, during the Buy More liquidation sale, but only later in the day, citing the need not to "scare anyone away too early" (vs. Ring Part II). Alas, he's right: the blanket-clad vaquero flashing demonic expressions and stoned pale face, complete with headdress and breastplate, prove an inspired background for the Intersect's 'high noon' duel in the middle of the night, but not likely one to move merchandise on the Buy More floor. Perhaps their lowest point comes outside the Buy More while playing on their break and a bystander offers them money…to stop playing (vs. Living Dead).

As their career proceeds, however, the reception of their work grows more welcoming. Though hauled out by police for trespassing and disturbing the peace at the hospital during Ellie's maternity visit, their polarizing performance of Salt-N-Pepa's "Push It" clearly resonates with several visitors, patients, and staff (vs. Push Mix). Even if the attempt ultimately fails to make Baby Clara's first encounter with music a live one, instead of "filtered…indie crap," the duo remains resolute in "shaping the youth of America...cover song by cover song." The highest praise comes when they go unplugged. After a blown amp forces them to play an impromptu, acoustic set in matching turtle necks at Devon and Ellie's going away party, their tender rendition of Peter, Paul and Mary's "Leaving on a Jet Plane" brings sincere applause. Additionally, the Woodcombs go to great lengths to steal the Sleep Sheep from the Buy More, on which Jeffster has installed a soothing, rolling Western-style tune that uniquely calms Baby Clara (vs. Masquerade).

Despite this epic combination of farces and promising glimpses, Jeffster's seemingly fused partnership still betrays a crack or two. In one regard, Lester sees himself as superior and periodically disdains Jeff. When Jeff voices some of his unfortunate, private thoughts, Lester typically complains, "Don't make me uncomfortable being with you" (vs. Marlin). But Lester's comments during the interrogation over Big Mike's missing marlin prove an even more vivid example. Blaming Jeff's "alcoholic ass" for sneaking into Big Mike's office for another drink in the first place, Lester blasts, "You're a disease! And you've diseased us all: Chuck, me, [Casey]." Though not made explicit until Season 5, the relationship is also based upon a power balance in which Lester exercises control over Jeff, who remains "subordinate" (vs. Hack Off). Indeed, Lester even deludes himself into believing that Jeff "like[s] being number two" (vs. Business Trip). Jeff's roles as Lester's mouthpiece during the Fight Club episode and butler/waiter/sitarist in the tent during the visit of the Hin-Jewess serve as prime examples of this paradigm. When Jeff steps out of that subservient role, problems arise.

The first evidence of this dynamic occurs on the musical front in a Season 3 event that foreshadows future problems. While playing on their break outside the Buy More (vs. Living Dead), a disagreement erupts over whether to retain Big Mike as band manager. Jeff favors the idea, thinking it will bring respect, while Lester ridicules the idea: "Art good; commercialism bad, evil, weird..chubby." Lester proceeds to test his control by vowing to "walk away" from "Jeffster": "You want his empty words and his razzmatazz wordplay, you take it. You take it and you go solo. And you see how that works out for you." Surprisingly, Jeff doesn't submit to his repeated threats, leaving Lester, who has backed himself into a corner, to take the "ster" with him.

Of course, Jeff's "lyrically lacking" solo career, which leaves at least one offended woman hurrying away in disgust, has all the markings of a short one. Lester, however, thinks otherwise, privately revealing his fears to Big Mike: "He'll be huge here; then he'll be huge in Japan. And then it's over." Initially, Lester rejects his potential manager's pep talk. When Big Mike claims, "You're more than just the 'ster' in "Jeffster; you're the 'stir' that stirs the drink," Lester replies, "I won't be fooled by corporate trickery. I will never bow down to 'The Man'." But after absorbing Big Mike's dream speech highlighting his brief turn as Rain with Earth, Wind, and Fire, Lester, moved to the point of tears, finally relents: "Where do I sign?" The split is avoided for the present, but concerns remain about their future.

When Jeff discovers sobriety and vital new capabilities in Season 5, the permanent alteration in the power balance of the relationship proves more than the careening acrobat can grasp. Predictably, a dark chapter in their relationship ensues. The issue comes to a head in "vs. Business Trip", when Lester has trouble drawing Jeff's attention away from the book he is reading to show him how he has falsified Buy More sales data in order to win the Salesman of the Year award and attend the convention in the Inland Empire. When Jeff confronts Lester, "Sometimes I think you are a bad person," adding, "Now undo what you've done," the scene ends with a bad omen: Lester's batting the book out of Jeff's hand. After the "fixed" competition winner is announced, Jeff subsequently squelches Lester's attempted populist revolt by countering with thankfulness for his job and a challenge to work harder, leaving Lester to withdraw with plotting eyes.

Indeed, after overhearing Dr. Woodcomb's diagnosis of the source of Jeff's mental problems and prescription for preventing their return, i.e. no more sleeping in the van and inhaling carbon monoxide fumes, the Hin-Jew settles on a scheme. Lester pumps the "poison" into the Buy More break room not primarily to murder Jeff but "keep [him] subordinate" by returning him to his formerly impaired state (vs. Hack Off). As Lester later clarifies, "I-I just needed you back, Man" (vs. Business Trip). Of course, not everyone has the resistance to carbon monoxide Jeff has accrued over years of exposure, so Jeff must wheel

Big Mike out before it's too late. When Lester shows no signs of remorse or desire for dialogue and even claims not to care that they are no longer friends, Jeff takes the first step in catching the tumbling trapeze artist before he plummets beyond anyone's grasp: having him arrested. As Jeff forthrightly explains, "I wish you were a better person. But unfortunately, you need to learn there are repercussions for your actions."

Lester's adjustment to the new status quo does not unfold overnight. In fact, matters become more strained as the penitentiary inmate actually stiffens his resistance to reform. Joining Jeff to visit Lester in prison, Morgan, in the wake of the disastrous Morgansect arc, attempts to empathize with Lester, but the Hin-Jew shows no signs of accepting an altered relational paradigm:

> **Morgan:** Recently I put some people that I care about through some rough times. That's the thing: true friendship is, it's confusing, isn't it?
>
> **Lester:** Just tell me what I have to do to get out of this place.
>
> **Morgan:** It's so simple. Jeff has agreed to drop all charges under one condition: you promise not to poison him anymore.
>
> **Lester:** Yeah, I'm sorry, I can't promise that.
>
> **Morgan:** Wake up, man! You are gonna get yourself killed in this!...Good luck in prison.
>
> **Lester:** No, good luck to you both finding a better Indian guy in your life or at the Buy More! I will see you both in hell! Which is just what I call "visiting hours".

With an assist from Morgan and the Indian Modeling Agency, Jeff not only stands his ground, but reaches out to catch his flailing friend with a lesson in tough love: "Scare Lester Straight". Accepting Morgan and Jeff's Skype request to chat, Lester initially interprets the gesture as Jeff's act of surrender: "I see you couldn't live without me." On the contrary, he is informed that interviews have been conducted to fill his spot at the Buy More. At first, Lester responds with sheer skepticism, that is until he meets the new Nerd Herder, Vali Chandrasekaren. Though Lester continues to laugh for a moment, criticizing the "pretty stupid name," his own moment of sobriety quickly follows. After asking, "Where are you from, Mr. Fake Name?" he doesn't receive an answer he was expecting. "Look at my face," his competition confidently smiles into the screen. "You can't tell I'm from Montreal, like all true Hin-Jews?" When Lester persists in disbelief, the True Hin-Jew adds injury to insult: "I did. And I am. I just wanted to say thanks for giving up your spot at the Buy More. Some great people here. I'm excited to start getting to know everybody." Before his friend has a chance to recover, Jeff delivers another savage blow: "Lester, you should hear this guy's singing voice. - Like an angel." Lester 2.0 proceeds to sing a few bars of "O Canada" in fluent French, leaving Lester 1.0 with mouth agape and nothing more to say than, "-My word." Finally, when Vali suggests his voice is the type "that would go perfectly with a...keytar," Lester folds, quietly asking, "May I have a moment alone with Jeffrey, please?" As Jeff later reports, Lester "changed his tune" as soon as he saw the "better Lester" and promises not to poison Jeff any more.

Upon Lester's return to the Buy More, he no longer controls the Jeffster relationship, allowing it to grow in a healthier manner. Accordingly, when they proceed with their final stalking mission of the series, discovering the Buy More is a cover for Carmichael Industries, it also serves as a metaphor that even Lester recognizes: "...Maybe this wasn't a search for a secret spy base. Maybe this was a search for friendship" (vs. Kept Man). Indeed, they work together, with Jeff taking the lead, to track down first Devon and then the rest of the Castle Crew, traveling as far as Colorado and the Vail Buy More in the process. In a sense, Jeff's punching through the fake wall with a dumb bell in the Buy More basement also serves as a figure for their collectively breaking through to a new, enlightened relationship as well as Jeff's individual improvement.

Still, this last chapter of their recorded journey together is not without its trials and tribulations. In one regard, the harsh reality they discover in the spy world, namely the firestorm of bullets in the Vail Buy More, leaves Jeffster quaking. No sooner does Lester confess, "I would like very much to forget everything, everything I saw here today," than Jeff claims himself "scarred, I'm so scarred" (vs. Bo), earning him a consoling rub of his back as he collapses on Lester's shoulder. In addition, they struggle to deal with the cycles of memory loss when Casey administers the short-term gas each time they decipher the secret identities of Chuck and company and mark their discoveries on their arms. Indeed, though they share the same dreams of fallen snow and a different Buy More, the prospect of someone "wip[ing] our memories clean" and "scour[ing] our minds" leaves Lester, once again, "scared" (vs. Bullet Train). So begins their final "call": to determine the truth "even if we have to face mortal danger."

As it turns out, the truth they discover includes not merely the true identities of others but their own identities as heroes as well. The sequence is set in motion when they pick up Morgan's "earling" from the parking lot asphalt to find Colonel Casey on the other end half a world away. With no one left in Burbank to help after Morgan and Devon are captured while failing to free Alex, a desperate Casey listens as Chuck, beside him on the bullet train, gives Jeffster his vote of confidence: "Look, I know this sounds crazy, but I've worked with those guys for years. They may seem like botulism victims, but they're loyal. They can do it." With no other option, Casey vows to Lester, "You do what I tell you, I'll make you a hero." Casey proceeds to send Jeffster to the Crown Vic, where they ignore his directive to leave "the big stuff" and grab the flame throwers. Part-Terminator and part-Rambo, a cigar-chomping Lester serves as the magnet for the flu bus henchman. Meanwhile, Jeff positions himself behind, cowing Quinn's minion even while ironizing Big Mike's opening question with a bold proclamation: "Behold the flames of destiny!" As a reward for their "miracle", Jeffster is granted their relatively humble demand as repayment: honesty about the Castle Crew's double lives and a tour of its base.

Still basking in the crowning achievement of their espionage career, Jeffster also attains its greatest musical achievement before the series fades to black. Backed by the symphony at the Pacific Concert Hall, they cover A-ha's "Take on Me" to the tune of a standing ovation, earning them a recording contract and tour in Germany (vs. Goodbye). While the pop anthem clearly links to Chuck's series finale plight as he seeks to salvage his relationship with an amnesiac Sarah, the lyrics equally apply to these partners, who take the risk of trusting each other even as they evolve as individuals. Accordingly, when they leave the Buy More for the final time, en route to the adoration of both "women and men" in Germany, the flat screens they pass project them as 'pardners' riding off into the sunset. Within this context, Jeffster's Halloween turn as the

"American Gothic" couple in Season 1 takes on an added dimension, for it ultimately serves as a complementary, foreshadowing image of their journey together. Married to one another in more than just name, Jeffster, similar to both cowboys and prairie farmers, leaves Burbank to forge a new frontier, one that they will face together.

CHAPTER 16: A "CHUCK" MOVIE

Completing the Text

In a January 2014 interview with Tim Stack of *Entertainment Weekly*, "Chuck" co-creator Josh Schwartz contrasted any potential "Chuck" movie with one that actually followed the conclusion of the "Veronica Mars" television series. Whereas "Veronica Mars" used a movie to wrap up telling a story it was not able to finish when denied a fourth season, Schwartz explained, "I think we'd really wanna make sure we had the right story to tell....We ended the show. We felt really good about where we ended it." The implication of this statement is that any "Chuck" movie would need to tell a new story, because the original one was complete.

From the standpoint of literary analysis, that proposition remains open to question. By series' end, a pair of key scenarios, metaphorically foreshadowed over five seasons, never materialize. Moreover, a couple of the finale's themes, one of them unresolved, beg for further exploration. Aside from these significant items of seemingly unfinished business, it wouldn't hurt to clear up a couple of persistent ambiguities either, just for curiosity's sake. In short, if a "Chuck" movie is ever produced, it should prioritize the completion and embellishment of the original literary text while interweaving any new storyline.

As argued in the first *Unpacking "Chuck"* (Chapter 12: Wandering into the Promised Land), the series loosely reprises the epic story of the Old Testament to structure the saga of Chuck and Sarah's romance. However, by series' end the climax of this sequence is still missing. Demonstrating this omission requires context, so let's review.

The series opens with a nondescript nerd quietly shepherding a flock of Nerd Herders when he is "chosen" to receive an unexpected email attachment, the Intersect. This event radically alters his life, partly by crossing his path with that of his future wife, who just happens to be named Sarah. For those not tracking, Chuck initially recalls Abraham in the biblical book of Genesis. A relatively ordinary shepherd with a wife named Sarah, Abraham is minding his own business when unexpectedly selected by God to receive a special covenant in which, ultimately, he will not only inherit a Promised Land, but become the father "of a great nation" so blessed that "all the families of the earth shall be blessed" through it (Gen. 12: 1-3). For good measure, the biblical Sarah laughs incredulously when told she will bear a son, a detail echoed in Agent Walker's initial ambivalence about having children.

Like Abraham's descendants, Chuck and Sarah at first languish in an Egyptian captivity of sorts: the invisible prison of handler/asset protocol. Indeed, for two seasons, with the brief exception of "vs. First Date," their professional relationship prevents them from exploring their feelings for one another until they embark on a nocturnal flight into the desert, i.e. Barstow, with Colonel Casey in hot pursuit. Similarly, the Hebrews fled Egypt by night with Pharaoh's army rushing after them, escaping into the Sinai Peninsula.

However, Chuck and Sarah, when finally free to pursue their "real" relationship, experience a bewildering turn of events, beginning with Sarah's initial cold feet at the Woodcomb wedding and continuing with Chuck's subsequent and ironic prioritization of the spy life over running with Sarah in Prague. Though it only seems like forty years, the Castle Couple spends the better half of Season 3 meandering in an emotional and psychological wilderness that imitates the Israelites' desert wandering. Moreover, during the course of Chuck and Sarah's estrangement, they commit 'idolatry' when redirecting the affections they pledged to one another (think charm bracelet) towards others (i.e. Hannah and Shaw), notably starting in an episode featuring a golden calf---er, mask---on loan from a Middle Eastern museum, no less. Before they exit The Wilderness, they must also first pass through the deep waters of Chuck's Red Test (i.e. Red Sea), a term pointedly with no basis in the real espionage world. Moreover, Chuck's passage of that test comes in a substitutionary manner when Casey secretly pulls the trigger on Chuck's behalf, suggesting the reprieve of Jacob, Abraham's son, from sacrificing his son Isaac after a ram is provided on Isaac's behalf. Even then, Chuck must eliminate Shaw on a Paris bridge in order to cross the erstwhile Jordan River (the

Seine suffices), and pass over into his personal Promised Land with Sarah: exclusive dating, engagement and ultimately marriage.

So how is "Chuck" not complete when it comes to the series' central romance? The answer is not primarily linked with whether Sarah gets her memories back, with a Magical Kiss or otherwise. Rather, key fulfillments of the Abrahamic Covenant have either still not yet come to pass or remain in question when the curtain falls on "Chuck", even if Chuck and Sarah indeed still inhabit their Promised Land and face the hazy horizon of the future together (as I argue in *Unpacking "Chuck"* Chapter 20: Prism Express). True, Chuck and Sarah prove a blessing to a dangerous world in need over five seasons through their collective use/protection of the Intersect. Still, struggling Carmichael Industries has not flourished: Sarah's plan to make it a family-friendly, cyber-oriented business never gets beyond the champagne she has chilling in Castle before Quinn abducts her, and there are still plenty of Philistines lying in wait out there, including financial ones.

In an even more significant sense, though, Chuck and Sarah have anticipated moving into the Dream House and starting a family, as emphasized in the drawing Chuck sketches on the Bullet Train. However, this never becomes reality either. The closing scenario falls a bit short of their metaphorically becoming a great nation that blesses others, given that they—assuming they still are a couple—remain childless and without a clear legacy. Finishing the text involves addressing these issues in a manner that at least indicates their ultimate fulfilment.

Chuck and Sarah's journey is not the only one that fails to reach its metaphorical destination. Jeff and Lester make their own pilgrimages, both individually and collectively, from depravity to nobility, but one last step remains for them as well. Their comical *cover* band identity also serves as a serious figure linked to their characterization from Season 1 through the beginning of Season 5, when abuse and fear, respectively, succeed in masking their personal potentials from the outside world (For more on these foibles see Chapters 4 & 8). As the series nears a close, those 'covers' are removed to reveal a destiny no one would have expected (See Chapter 15: The Flames of Destiny). Evidencing such phenomenal growth, Jeffster should no longer be associated with covering the creations of others. Instead, the metaphor should be completed by having them create and perform their own original music. This scenario presents a wonderful opportunity for the duo's first non-cover hit to be released and performed in conjunction with a world tour.

The series also closes with a pair of themes either not fully resolved or explored. In the case of the former, Chuck ends the series in a distinctly ironic situation concerning the Intersect (See Chapter 2: The Trials of Dr. Jibb). After coming to the conclusion that the secret government program embodies more a curse than a blessing, Chuck agrees with his father's prior assessment that it needs to be destroyed. But when the screen fades to black on that Malibu Beach, the show ends with the paradoxical entity still inhabiting Chuck's head, somehow having found him once again. A "Chuck" movie presents the chance to destroy it once and for all, ridding Chuck of the 'curse' that follows him with a seeming mind of its own. Alternatively, the idea could be reconfigured, with the Intersect changing his mind to see the blessings of the Intersect outweighing its hazards, or even possibly finding a way to separate one from the other and destroy the evil element.

On a more uniformly positive note, a "Chuck" movie also stands poised with a delicious opportunity to make manifest a theme emphasized in the final episode. In express fashion, an even more cynical and fearful Sarah than her Season 1 counterpart falls in love with Chuck all over again (See *Unpacking 'Chuck'* Chapter 20: Prism Express). By faith, she is able to see her true identity as Mrs. Sarah Bartowski through the prism of Chuck's sacrificial love, though unable to recall the tangible evidences of that identity surrounding her. What greater delight could await the viewer than to see Sarah's progressive wonder at the depth of that devoted love, as well as Chuck's ability to once again share their romantic legacy, as she experiences a series of reawakenings to former feelings that enrich her new ones and confirm the trust she has placed in Chuck?

Think of the potentialities. Spotting the charm bracelet in a jewelry box followed by a rush of images, including Chuck crouched before her in the Buy More and it dangling from her wrist as she protects their future by pulling the trigger on Mauser. Or the sight of her red trench coat hanging in a closet, triggering a flashback to muzzle flashes on a Paris bridge, and her salvation while drugged from Shaw by Chuck. How about a passing reference to Decker or The Norseman that suddenly returns her to a hospital bed with Chuck holding her hand as she regains consciousness on the eve of their wedding because of his relentless delivery of an antidote? The possibilities are endless, and far more satisfying than downloading memories from Intersect glasses or finding the Magical Kiss worked. However, one image remains non-negotiable: Sarah herself said that she would "never forget" the drawing of them holding a baby in front of the Dream Home (vs. Bullet Train). The omission of the sketch from the finale is inexplicable.

Then there are those nagging ambiguities that inquiring minds simply want to have clarified. One mystery that persists through the finale is the nature of Orion's relationship with Bryce Larkin and what their apparent collaboration on the Omaha Project looked like. This would shed more insight on the dynamics of Chuck's time both during his years at and following Stanford all the way up to his receipt of the Intersect in the Pilot. Furthermore, it would enable both deceased characters to join in on the reunion through creative discovery of video logs and the like.

Finally, and surely most controversially, a "Chuck" movie presents the chance to blind side an audience while offering a radical yet consistent redemptive message. Every major character still living at series' end evidences some positive growth, even villains like Heather Chandler, Jill Roberts and especially Vladimir Volkoff. All except for one prominent traitor, sealed in a cell hopefully no future virus will ever unlock again. How profound and unexpected would it be if the most hated character in the series at last joined the others and experienced his own epiphany, either before performing a dramatic atoning gesture or after finding himself the recipient of a transforming grace?

Viewed from a distance as a whole, the 5-season text of "Chuck" coalesces into an impressive mosaic. Hopefully, an opportunity will arise to embellish it by inserting additional pieces, some of which are still missing.

26943583R00093

Made in the USA
Middletown, DE
08 December 2015